Palaces

arsenale e&t editrice

Photographs by Mark Smith.
All of these documents come from
the collection of Arsenale Editrice, Venice.

© Éditions Hazan, Paris, 1998
Editor: Éric Reinhardt
assisted by Margherita Castellani
Design: Atalante
Production: Muriel Landsperger
Color separation: Seleoffset, Torino
Printing: Milanostampa, Farigliano

ISBN: 2 85025 607 2
ISSN : 1275-5923
Printed and Bound in Italy

Venetian Palaces

Translated from Italian
by Simon Pleasance
and Fronza Woods

POCKET ✷ ARCHIVES

HAZAN

Introduction

For Marcel Proust, an enchanted garden, for Byron, a place of poetry, and for Pierre Auguste Renoir, a promised land – Venice has always attracted poets and artists, who have ventured spellbound into its mysterious and meandering streets, byways, and canals.

Chateaubriand, Hemingway, Mozart, Monet, Goethe, Turner, and the names of many other illustrious foreign travellers are interwoven with those of the city's ancient families, of palaces smacking of the Orient, and of hidden nooks and crannies well off the beaten track.

The origins of Venice, an important center of European literary and poetic culture, date back to the period when the Lombards invaded the Italic peninsula. At the time, the islands and rare areas of terra firma, which emerged from the brackish waters and the canebrakes, were peopled by inhabitants of the inland Roman townships. It is this very place that later became known as of the Venetian and Friulian region. The first doge was elected in 697, and the last one abdicated exactly 1100 years later when, in 1797, Napoleon decreed the end of the Venetian Republic, the Serenissima.

Legend has it that it was Saint Peter who ordered the Rialto community to build a basilica in his honour on the island of Olivolo, which was subsequently called Castello. What is more, the twelve Apostles, the Virgin Mary, and Jesus Christ himself wanted a church in the new city, and so it was that the first places of worship sprang up on those islands in the middle of the lagoon.

Bricks and pieces of stone coming from older sites on terra firma were often used to build the ecclesiastical buildings, but the earliest dwellings, erected along the channels on a layer of clay and sand – the so-called *caranto* – were made of timber. The foundations were made of mud, consolidated with burnt marsh reeds, criss-crossed planks of larch wood, and boulders.

In the twelfth and thirteenth centuries, however, by which time many buildings had been damaged and destroyed by major fires, timber was gradually replaced by more fire-resistant materials, such as dressed stone, brick – which caused the nineteenth-century poet Alfred de Musset to refer to the city as Venise La Rouge – and white marble, the so-called stone of Istria.

From this period on, the Venetian Gothic style, much-extolled by John Ruskin in his book *The Stones of Venice*, started to develop. The main features of this style were pointed arches, mullioned windows with several lights, and the interplay of colored marble. As such, the style clearly reveals the Byzantine influence stemming from the political ties – to start with, the doge was nothing more than a vassal of the emperor of Byzantium – and the trading links that Venice had established with the Orient. Today, sadly, little remains of the bright multi-colored effects that were typical of the Venetian Gothic style.

In the thirteenth century, the first monumental private buildings were designed, such as the large Palazzo dei Pesaro, subsequently known as the Fondaco dei Turchi, and the traditional typology of the Venetian palace was drawn up. With its three-part plan, its function as a residence was combined with that of offices and warehouses. The main façade, with its distinctive central group of windows, invariably gave onto a canal; the entrance hall, stretching from one end of the building to the other and thus giving access to it from both land and water, was flanked by large storehouses on the ground floor; and on the upper floor there were various rooms along the central *portego*.

In the centuries that followed, the architects Mauro Codussi and Jacopo Sansovino reinterpreted these typical features of Venice's Gothic palaces in a Renaissance key, Baldassare Longhena introduced the Baroque taste, and Giannantonio Selva continued to use these Gothic features but adapted them to the neo-classical style. The large number of palaces is a direct result of the burgeoning nobility and the far-reaching branches of the various families. Down the centuries, the various lines of the Contarini family, for example, built more than twenty-five palaces. In order to distinguish the various residences from one another, they were named by combining the family name with a word indicating a specific characteristic of the building or of the family branch itself.

The aristocracy of the Serenissima was not permitted to confer upon itself titles other than *N.H., nobilis homo,* and *N.D., nobil donna.* The title of *Messer*, on the other hand, could only be used by the procurators of San Marco, the only lifelong office apart from that of the *cancellier grande* and the dogeship.

The patriciate wielded its power through the constitutional organ of the Maggior Consiglio, which was established at the end of the thirteenth century, and which consisted of noblemen of more than twenty-five years of age.

In the fourteenth century, the city of Venice had some one hundred thousand inhabitants, and out of one hundred patrician families, only thirty were part of the closed circle of "grandees" and extremely wealthy aristocratic families. Yet the Venetian nobility never flaunted its wealth, not least because certain laws put a limit on excessive luxury and pomp.

The amount of the dowries of young patrician brides, the number of courses at nuptial banquets, and the quantity of silk and jewels owned were all precisely stipulated by the Maggior Consiglio. In fact, because the Consiglio granted them just a few yards of precious fabrics each year, Venetian noblewomen avoided spoiling their clothes by wearing very high shoes in which they were only able to walk at a snail's pace, supporting themselves on the heads of two servants.

Likewise, the dimensions of the palaces and the presence of decorative elements on the façades were governed by strict standards, as was the number of tapestries and brocades hanging inside.

Nowadays few palaces still belong to the descendants of those age-old proprietors. Most of the patrician families have died out or moved elsewhere, and very few of the surviving families have preserved the heritage of a bygone era. Many palaces have been turned into hotels, some house public and private offices, and others have been divided up into apartments.

For all this, Venice has lost none of its charm, and the rooms of some palaces still reverberate today with balls and parties organized in honour of some famous guest who had come from afar to drink from, and get drunk on, the magical atmosphere of this city.

1 - Palazzo Albrizzi

The Albrizzi family, hailing from Bergamo, settled in Venice in the sixteenth century, where they became extremely wealthy from the textile trade and oils. Admitted to the Consiglio Maggiore (Higher Council) in 1667, they signed and sealed their introduction to the patriarchate, once and for all, by purchasing the Palazzo Bonomo, located on the Rio di San Cassiano.

The formal, austere façade of the palace is hallmarked by its windows, which are protected by small roof-like structures carved in stone. Judging from its architectural plan, one would conclude that this façade was probably decorated with frescoes. The sober exterior contrasts with the sumptuous decoration inside the palace, which includes stucco décors, multicolored rooms, the white-and-gold extravagance of the *portego*, the *putti* and cupids supporting the family coat of arms, and the ceiling paintings on canvas by Antonio Pellegrini. The walls are hung with pictures by Pietro Liberi and Antonio Zanchi, as well as a portrait of the Albrizzi family by Pietro Longhi. It was in 1771 that the Albrizzis had several small houses behind the palace pulled down in order to enlarge it, the outcome being the present-day Campiello Albrizzi. This residence was then one of the most sought-after palaces in Venice. In that period, Isabella Teotochi, wife of Giuseppe Albrizzi and lady of the house, held a famous literary salon frequented by Vittorio Alfieri, Vincenzo Monti, Antonio Canova, Lord Byron – who called her the Madame de Staël of Venice – and Ugo Foscolo, who, by all accounts, felt something more powerful than mere platonic friendship for Isabella. The Teatro Nuovo di San Cassiano, the theatre where Claudio Monteverdi's musical dramas were staged, stood near the palace. It was destroyed in 1812, which gave the Albrizzis the opportunity to extend the gardens. Today the descendants of the Albrizzi family still live in this palace .

2 - Palazzo Balbi

Legend has it that the Palazzo Balbi was built out of "spite." The story goes that Nicolò Balbi was living in a rented house. On one occasion, he forgot to pay his rent on time and was stopped in the street by his landlord, who rudely upbraided him for his oversight. Enraged by this unexpected insult, Nicolò resolved to have a house built for himself as quickly as possible on a plot of land that he owned. In the meantime, however, he had no desire to continue as a tenant of the man who had so offended him, and he took his entire family off to live on a large boat, which he moored right in front of the windows of his former landlord, thus depriving the house of daylight. True or not, the legend does in a way explain the speed with which Alessandro Vittoria built this palace between 1582 and 1590. The Balbi di San Pantalon family, which claimed descent from the ancient Balba clan that came to Rome from Spain, was noteworthy above all for its culture. Luigi put together a huge library and a music room, Gasparo was a well-reputed cosmographer and traveller, and Adriano was a noted late-eighteenth-century geographer.

It was from the loggia on the Mannerist façade of this palace that Napoleon watched the regatta organized in his honour on 2 December 1807.

The historical origins of the regatta date back to 1315, when the doge Soranzo ordained a series of festivities to mark the arrival of the queen of Sicily. Then, as now, the famous rowing races finished in front of the Palazzo Balbi where temporary festive structures were built for the occasion.

In 1887 the palace was sold to the Jewish antiquarian Michelangelo Guggenheim. Twenty-six years later, the antiquarian auctioned off his collections, and the palace was subsequently bought by the Adriatica Electricity Company. Today it is the seat of the Veneto Regional Council.

3 - Palazzo Barbarigo della Terrazza

The fame of this palace is bound up with an outstanding period art collection that included paintings by Giorgione, Titian, Tintoretto, Giulio Romano, and many other sixteenth and seventeenth-century masters. It was Cristoforo Barbarigo who purchased the pictures by Titian in 1581, for they had remained in the artist's house after his death in 1576.

In 1850 the most important works were bought by Czar Nicholas I. Today they are the pride of the Hermitage in Saint Petersburg. The palace, with its distinctive terrace over the Grand Canal, is attributed to Bernardino Contin, who built it between 1568 and 1569 for Andrea Barbarigo, who was known as the Bank. When the Serenissima (the Venetian Republic) fell, the sole remaining heir was the senator Giovanni Filippo, who bequeathed the palace to a distant relative, Count Nicolò Giustinian; who in turn sold the lot.

The palace passed through various hands and even housed the writer Gabriele d'Annunzio for all of three days in 1921. Today it is home to the German Center of Venetian Studies.

4 - Palazzo Barbaro

This palace, which was once the Barbaro family residence on the Grand Canal, is made up of two adjacent buildings: one Gothic, attributed to Giovanni Bon, and the other tending towards the Baroque, built by Antonio Gaspari.

The eighteenth-century ballroom was renowned for its ceiling decorations by Giambattista Tiepolo, which are now in safekeeping in the New York Metropolitan Museum. The library – an obvious necessity for a family of scholars and men of letters, and lovers and students of art, such as the Barbaros – was no less famous.

Ermolao Barbaro, a well-known philologist, commentator on Pliny, and Aristotelian scholar, was appointed patriarch of Aquileia in 1491; as was his great-grandson Daniele, likewise a philosopher, mathematician, keen astronomer, and translator of Vitruvius. In 1560, along with his brother Marc' Antonio, ambassador at Constantinople during the War of Cyprus, Daniele commissioned Andrea Palladio to design the famous Villa Barbaro in Maser and Paolo Veronese to decorate it. Both artists were their close friends and protégés. It was Marc' Antonio who saved Veronese's life when he was found guilty of irreverence by the Holy Office, for having painted a Last Supper for the Convent of Santi Giovanni e Paolo that was deemed too worldly. Barbaro had the bright idea of changing the title, thus turning the Last Supper into the *Feast in the House of Levi*.

After a dazzling eighteenth century, with the Republic no longer holding sway, the impoverished Barbaros fell on hard times and were forced to sell their residence.

In 1885 a cultured and sophisticated Bostonian couple, the Curtises, purchased the palace from its then current owners. At Ca' Barbaro, the Curtises received writers and artists, including Robert Browning, John Singer Sargent, Isabella Stewart Gardner, and Henry James who, during one of his long stays in this palace, wrote *The Aspern Papers*. In the autumn of 1908, the painter Claude Monet and his wife Alice also disembarked at the palace. Henry James' novel *The Wings of the Dove* contains a description of the rooms in which the descendants of the Curtises still live to this day: "... the warmth of the Southern summer was still in the high florid rooms, palatial chambers where hard cool pavements took reflexions in their lifelong polish, and where the sun on the stirred sea-water, flickering up through open windows, played over the painted 'subject' in the splendid ceiling..."

The two buildings compose the Barbaro Palace.

5 - Palazzo Belloni Battagia

With its elongated doors and windows, the Palazzo Belloni Battagia, which was built between 1647 and 1663, invokes memories of the Gothic palace. At the same time, however, the architect Baldassare Longhena implemented an obvious seventeenth-century touch, which is characterized in the broken pediment and the two large coats of arms with half moons and emblematic stars that embellish the principal floor. The high cost of the palace and the attendant financial problems forced the Belloni family to lease out the palace, shortly after work on it had finished, to the Austrian ambassador Count Czernin. The palace was later purchased, first by the Battagia family, and in 1804, by the merchant Antonio Capovilla, who enlarged it by adding several rooms and a garden. After changing hands several times since, the main floor of the building now belongs to the Foreign Trade Institute, while the remainder of the palace is designed for private use.

6 - Palazzo Bembo

It would seem that the poet-cum-cardinal Pietro Bembo, man of letters and historian, friend of Lucrezia Borgia and Caterina Corner, as well as secretary to Pope Leo X, never actually resided in this Gothic palace on the Riva del Carbon.

The Bembo family had come to Venice from Bologna and had taken part in the election of the first doge in 697. The lineage of San Salvador, owner of this palace, is mentioned in the Saint Mark's codex *Casi infelici, fini e Morte di Nobili Veneti* (Hapless Events, the End and Death of Venetian Nobles), on account of the physical deformities that recurred among its members. Between the early sixteenth century and the mid-seventeenth century, five deformed Bembos were recorded: Lorenzo, Francesco, and Zuanne Maria were all born lame, Domenico was a hunchback, and Piero was "extremely frail."

In the autumn of 1510, Giuliano de'Medici betook himself to Venice to find a cure for his ophthalmia, and stayed in this palace.

7 - Palazzo Bernardo

The two entrance portals clearly show us that this Gothic palace was once the residence of two families belonging to the same house. The Palace dates from the mid-fifteenth century, and it is to this period that most of the two-family Gothic buildings can be traced (see, for example, the Giustinian palaces).

On various occasions, the Bernardo residence was host to famous figures who came to Venice at the invitation of the Republic, and during these visits the Bernardos would retire to another part of the palace. The more illustrious guests included Francesco Sforza and Bianca Visconti, who stayed here in 1442, when the building must have been only just completed.

8 - Palazzo dei Camerlenghi

The Palazzo dei Camerlenghi, so named after the magistrates who presided over the treasury of the Serenissima, was one of the first palaces in Europe to be specifically earmarked for offices. Built between 1525 and 1528 where the previous seat of the Camerlenghis had stood, the building is attributed to Guglielmo de'Grigi. In addition to the offices of the Republic's treasurers, the palace also housed the prison and the merchants' arcade.

It was the custom among the magistrates who were at the end of their term, to leave as a gift, a painting that integrated either their coat of arms or their portrait into a religious theme. These works are now in the Gallerie dell'Accademia and the Cini Foundation.

There is a strange anecdote regarding two carved figures that decorate the façade of this palace. Towards the end of the sixteenth century, when the Rialto bridge was still a wooden structure, there had been several plans to rebuild it in stone, and it had been primarily the reservations of the Camerlenghis over the cost of such a project that had postponed the work. The populace was divided into two schools of thought over the idea: some maintained that the bridge would have to be renovated sooner or later; others claimed that it would never need replacing. This latter opinion was shared by an elderly couple, who found themselves drinking in the Rialto tavern. They became so enraged by those holding the opposite view, that the old man exclaimed: "If there's to be a new bridge, I want a claw to spring from my thighs!" The old lady chimed in: "And I want my buttocks to be set on fire!" Allusion to these somewhat special wishes was apparently made by Guglielmo de'Grigi, when he carved a huddled man with a claw-clad foot between his legs, and on the opposite pilaster a seated woman with her vagina ablaze.

At the present time this palace is the seat of the Audit Office.

9 - Palazzo Coccina Giunti Foscarini Giovanelli

No trace remains today of the Paolo Veronese frescoes that once decorated the main façade of this palace, which gives on to the Grand Canal. The frescoes on the façade of the inner courtyard appear to have been painted by Gian Battista Zelotti. Ownership of the Gothic building, which was rebuilt in the latter half of the eighteenth century, was transferred from the Coccina family to the Giunti family, who were famous Florentine printers and publishers, and then to the Foscarinis.

The fearsome event that befell Antonio Foscarini, erstwhile ambassador at the courts of the king of France and the king of England, is still fresh in people's memories today. In 1622 he was discovered dead, suspended by one foot, from a gibbet. The rumour spread swiftly abroad that the nobleman's tragic death had to do with his amorous liaison with the countess Alathea of Arundel and Surrey, consort of the Earl Marshal of England. It is believed that Antonio Foscarini was clandestinely proceeding, alone and armed, to the Palazzo Mocenigo at San Samuele, residence of the countess. As fate would have it, however, the plenipotentiary of the Medicis, the secretary of the imperial ambassador, and the secretary of the Spanish ambassador, all just happened to be staying at the Palazzo Mocenigo, too.

The prosecution did not dwell on the amorous grounds for the nobleman's visit, but had him arrested on suspicion of holding secret meetings with the representatives of hostile foreign powers. To save the honour of his beloved Alathea, Foscarini did not own up to the real reason for his nocturnal intrusions. He ended up strangled in prison and his corpse was publicly hanged.

This event caused a considerable stir in seventeenth-century Venice. And two centuries later, the dramatist Gian Battista Niccolini even wrote a tragedy about the unjust verdict handed down to Antonio Foscarini.

10 - Palazzo Coccina Tiepolo Papadopoli

In the 1860s, a period of anti-Austrian sentiment stemming from a desire for independence and for Italian unity, this palace played a leading role in all of twelve raids carried out by the Austrian authorities who governed Venice at that time. Mrs. Maddalena Montalban, who was in fact residing in the building, was well-known for her political commitment to "the revolution." She had been arrested once in 1860 for having aided and abetted various young people in making good their clandestine flight. In 1863 she was accused of high treason for selling objects with political connotations, collecting money for the "subversive party," and commissioning a ceremonial sword of honour for General Garibaldi. In addition to all this, she had promised to give an album to Princess Maria Pia of Savoy on the occasion of her marriage to the prince of Portugal. Fortunately for her, she was sentenced to just one year in prison. When Vittorio Emanuele II entered Venice in 1866, he was keen to express his gratitude to her in person, which he did by taking her hand and offering her a piece of jewelry.

The palace was built in approximately 1560 by Giangiacomo de'Grigi for the Coccina family, merchants who came originally from Bergamo and collectors of important works of art. Most notably, their collection included four paintings by Paolo Veronese, which are now in the Gemäldegalerie in Dresden.

When the Coccinas died out, the residence passed on to the Tiepolos in 1748, and in 1837, to Valentino Comello, husband of Maddalena Montalban. After changing hands several more times, the counts Aldobrandini-Papadopoli bought it in 1864. They added a garden and a new wing to the original palace, and also redecorated the interior.

Since 1922 the palace has belonged to the counts Arrivabene.

11 - Palazzo Contarini dal Bovolo

This Gothic palace with its pointed arches takes its name from the unusual outer staircase which takes the form of a cylindrical tower that climbs like a spiral, or to use the Venetian dialect word that means spiral and snail, *bovolo*. Giovanni Contarini commissioned Giovanni Candi to build this stairway in order to link the outbuildings to the palace itself in1499.

In the eighteenth century, ownership of the place passed to the Minelli family, oil merchants who had been admitted to the Consiglio Maggiore (the Higher Council) in 1650, after offering the city the sum of one hundred thousand ducats.

In 1803, after several changes of ownership, the residence was bought by the hotelier Arnoldo Marseille. Today it is the headquarters of an organization called the Congregation of Charity, which runs the city's asylums and educational and training institutes.

12 - Palazzo Contarini degli Scrigni e Corfù

Like the Palazzo Barbaro, this palace is the result of the merging of two adjoining buildings that date back to different periods. The Gothic palace, known as Corfù, was built by Sire Piero Contarini, nicknamed Pinza d'Oro (Golden Pliers), towards the end of the fourteenth century; while work on the second edifice got under way in 1609, to a design by Vincenzo Scamozzi, and was completed in 1630.

The seventeenth-century building was joined to the Gothic dwelling in order to increase the number of reception rooms. The name of the more recently built palace, degli Scrigni, comes from the caskets that were found in the Contarini family's villa at Piazzola sul Brenta.

A memorable reception was given in the Palazzo Corfù in 1525 to mark the marriage of Paolo Contarini and Vienna Gritti, niece of Andrea, the famous doge who appears in many of Titian's paintings. The festivities were grandiose and went on for several days. After the religious ceremony and a grand ball in the Doge's Palace, the bride, accompanied by 113 bejewelled ladies, was taken on the doge's sumptuous galley, the Bucintoro or Bucentaur, to be transported via the Grand Canal to the bridegroom's palace, which had been lit by day.

On the death of the last descendant of the Contarinis, Count Girolamo, in the first half of the nineteenth century, the palace was inherited by his two grand-daughters, by the name of Venier. Subsequently, the palace passed into the hands of Countess Matilde Berthold, and is now owned by the counts Rocca. The valuable collection of pictures is now held in the Gallerie dell'Accademia di Belle Arti, while the collection of books and codices is housed in the Biblioteca Marciana (Saint Mark's Library).

13 - Palazzo Contarini delle Figure

The naturalistic character of the decorations of the main floor, the branches from which elegant panoplies bloomed, the trophies affixed to tree trunks; all these caused John Ruskin to remember this palace with a dash of melancholy. For him, it was as if the artist had wanted to portray the dying naturalism of Gothic art. With the advent of autumn, leaves fell... With the frost of the Renaissance, everything died.

Evidently, Ruskin's remarks were not inspired by the harmonious façade of the building that was rebuilt between 1504 and 1546 upon an already existing Gothic structure. This plan has been attributed to Antonio Abbondi, otherwise known as Scarpagnino, despite the fact that the decorative elements, the already Mannerist taste of the sculptures, and the tympanum over the central four-light window all reveal a culture that differs from Scarpagnino's Renaissance background.

The palace owes its name to the two sculptures set beneath the main balcony. According to popular tradition, one of the two half-figures depicts a desperate man tearing out his hair because he has gambled and lost everything he owns, including his own consort; while the other figure is the wife, beside herself with anger. Memories of this palace are associated in particular with Jacopo Contarini, a famous scholar whose areas of interest ranged from art to botany, and from architecture to mathematics. His collection of paintings included works by Bassano, Titian, Tintoretto, and Palma the Younger, while the library housed scientific tomes, drawings of ancient temples, and mathematical instruments. On top of this, his garden was renowned for its variety of tropical plants. His knowledge of architecture earned him the friendship of Andrea Palladio who, during his stays in Venice, was almost invariably put up in the palace, until 1570, when he moved in on a permanent basis. The Contarinis remained in possession of many of the architect's drawings, which are today held at the Royal Institute of British Architects in London.

When Henry III of France visited Venice, Jacopo was charged with co-organizing the festivities. He commissioned Palladio to build a triumphal arch inspired by the Arch of Septimus Severus, and Tintoretto to paint the portrait of the sovereign on the Bucentaur. In 1577 the senate gave him the task of drawing up the program of paintings for the great hall of the Consiglio Maggiore and the Scrutinio or Ballot Inspectorate, which had been destroyed by fire.

The last heir, Bertucci Contarini, died in 1712. The artworks, which included Veronese's famous *Rape of Europa,* were transferred to the Doge's Palace, and the building became the property of the Serenissima. Subsequently, in the nineteenth century, the palace was purchased by the marquises Guiccioli, whose family also included Alessandro Guiccioli, husband of Teresa. Incidentally, Teresa is better known as Lord Byron's last great love.

Today the palace is in private hands and has been divided up into apartments.

Opposite: the fireplace of one of the salons in the Palazzo Contarini delle Figure, with stucco silhouettes above.

14 - Palazzo Contarini Fasan

This diminutive Gothic palace, built in approximately 1450, has always been referred to by popular tradition as "Desdemona's house." Yet Othello's house has tended to be identified with the Palazzo Guoro in Campo dei Carmini. Perhaps because they sound alike, the surname Guoro was confused with that of the Moro family. Othello has in fact been tentatively identified with the patrician Cristoforo Moro, lieutenant governor of Cyprus, who took as his second wife a daughter of Donato da Lezze. She was known as the Dimonio Bianco (White Devil), and it was from this nickname that Giambattista Giraldi Cinthio derived the name Desdemona, heroine of his novella *Gli Hecatommithi* (1565), which in turn, was Shakespeare's source for his tragedy written in 1602. Thus arose the legend of a Moor named Othello, who had set sail for Cyprus as a valiant captain, and slain his wife Desdemona, member of a noble Venetian family, out of jealousy. However the daughter of Donato da Lezze did not end up strangled.

Othello and Desdemona were later identified as Nicola and Palma Querini, who were married in 1535, with a gap of thirteen years between their respective ages, just like Othello and Desdemona. Nicola was a soldier, and it is quite conceivable that he was Moorish, since many Venetians had Moorish blood in their veins at the time. Moreover, as late as 1902, a dark-skinned Querini was still in evidence. After the early years of their marriage, Nicola became wracked by fits of jealousy, due not least to his long periods away from home, waging war against the Turks. He started to abuse his consort to such a degree that she escaped his clutches and returned to her parents' home. Her parents then accused Nicola of having attempted to strangle his wife – but he received no more than a light punishment and was recalled to Venice. He was murdered twenty years later.

15 - Palazzo Contarini Flangini Fini

In 1638 the lawyer Tommaso Flangini purchased two separate houses at San Moisè from Giambattista Contarini, in order to build the palace which still stands here today. It seems more than likely that Pietro Bettinelli was put in charge of the project, in so much as his name shows up frequently in the Flanginis' bookkeeping papers between 1628 and 1645. Later on, Tommaso's daughter, Marietina, sold the building to the Finis, possibly when she and her husband Benedetto Soranzo decided to go and live in the new palace of San Geremia.

The Fini family came originally from Cyprus, and had amassed a huge fortune from trade. They had been settled in Venice for quite some time when they were included among the city's patrician families in 1649. In the latter half of the seventeenth century, they had the palace on the Grand Canal modernized and largely rebuilt. The most reliable hypothesis is that it was Alessandro Tremignon who carried out the work, for he had been commissioned by the family to design the extremely ornate façade of San Moisè. Changes in ownership and the conversion of the palace into a hotel brought an end to the eighteenth-century luxury of the interior decorations. Indeed, the stucco-framed paintings, the gilded panels decorated with multi-colored motifs, and much of the furniture have all been scattered. The hotel that did business here in the nineteenth century was called the Grand Hôtel, and it welcomed John Ruskin during one of his long stays in Venice.

Today the palace, which is said to be built on trunks of cedar, is the property of the Veneto Region and houses the Regional Council.

16 - Palazzo Contarini Polignac dal Zaffo

In the days of the Serenissima, as the Republic was known, this palace was called the Palazzo Contarini dal Zaffo alla Carità, the word Zaffo derived from the city of Jaffa. The Contarinis were wealthy landowners with several estates in the Near East, and because they were unable to confer upon themselves the title of Lords of Jaffa, they decided to attach the name Zaffo to their own. The Contarinis, who took part in the election of the first doge in 697, were one of the oldest families in Venice. Their roots go right back to the Roman Aurelia Cotta clan, which was the family of Caesar's mother. They became prefects of the Rhine and their name is probably a contracted form of Cotta Rheni (counts of the Rhine).

We know nothing about the earliest owners of this palace, which was acquired by the Contarini dal Zaffo family in the latter half of the sixteenth century. The palace, which was probably built in the late fifteenth century was in fact attributed to both Mauro Codussi and Giovanni Buora. At the end of the eighteenth century, Giandomenico Tiepolo covered the rooms with rich decorations, but unfortunately, only a few fragments of this work have survived to this day.

Towards the end of the eighteenth century, the residence was sold to Domenico Manzoni, a silk merchant, and in the early twentieth century, after changing hands several times, the palace was bought by the princess of Polignac. The princess of Polignac was not only a connoisseur and patron of the arts, but also a painter and musician, herself. She enjoyed the friendship of Sargent and Picasso, and her salon on the Grand Canal was every bit a match for the most celebrated European salons of the day.

Nowadays the palace is the property of the descendants of the duke of Decazes.

17 - Palazzo Corner della Ca' Granda

On 16 August 1532 a devastating fire totally destroyed the Palazzo Malombra at San Maurizio, the residence that Giorgio Corner, brother of the queen of Cyprus, had purchased from Bartolomeo Malombra for twenty thousand ducats.

"It could have been the fire of Troy," noted the diarist Marin Sanudo, "for nothing was left standing, except for the tips of the columns; everything else was burnt and ruined." The cause of this disaster was coal fires in the rooms on the topmost floor, lit to dry out a large consignment of sugar that had just arrived from Cyprus. The heat from the embers beneath the dry beams of the attic set the wooden structure alight and nobody noticed. "Fire in Ca' Corner!" The cry echoed along the Grand Canal, while the top floor of the palace blazed. The fire then spread. Seventy beds were destroyed, along with the chapel, the paintings in the *portego*, the sugar, and four hundred bushels of wheat. Work on the rebuilding of the palace, to a design by Jacopo Sansovino, got under way in 1533, and it appears to have been completed by Scamozzi some time after 1556.

When Sansovino planned the Palazzo Corner della Ca' Granda, he introduced both Tuscan and Roman Renaissance features into the city of Venice: the sweeping courtyard, the large oval windows with scroll frames, and the large voluted corbels.

The palace remained in the hands of the Corners until 1812, when the last descendant, Niccolò, who was very much in favour of French-style democracy, sold it to the State Property Office. The interior was stripped of its furnishings, books, and paintings, which included works by Tintoretto, Raphael, and Titian. Just a few ceilings are all that is left of the original decoration. Under Austrian rule, the building became the seat of the Imperial and Royal Provincial Delegation. After the unification of Italy, it became, and remains, the seat of the Prefecture.

18 - Ca' Corner della Regina

It was here, in 1454, that the famous queen of Cyprus, Caterina Cornaro, wife of Jacques II of Lusignan, was born.

Jacques II was the illegitimate son of King Jean II, and he had taken the throne of Cyprus over the legitimate heir Charlotte, wife of Louis of Savoy. Afraid that attempts might be made to avenge this ousting from power and worried by a possible attack by the Turks, Jacques resolved to find a Venetian wife in order to strengthen the bonds of friendship that he entertained with the Serenissima. Marco Corner had a thirteen-year-old daughter who, in accordance with the codes and criteria of the Renaissance, was of marriageable age. A portrait of the girl, Caterina, was instantly dispatched, and legend has it that, when the king set eyes on it, he fell madly in love with her. Thus on 31 July 1468 their marriage by proxy was celebrated in Venice, with much pomp and circumstance. Caterina was adopted by the Serenissima as a daughter of the Republic, an honour never before bestowed on anyone before her, and the State contributed to her dowry, which amounted to one hundred thousand gold ducats. Four whole years elapsed before the queen was allowed to set off for her new kingdom, accompanied by a magnificent cortège. She was crowned queen of Cyprus, Jerusalem and Armenia in the cathedral of Famagusta. However the marriage was short-lived. "King Zaco" (Zaco, derived from Jacques) passed away in July 1473, leaving Caterina marooned and expecting a child. On his deathbed, the king left his wife the entire inheritance of the Lusignan dynasty, and she would indeed have reigned over his kingdom, assisted by a council of regents. But shortly after Jacques' death, she fell into the hands of a group of conspirators who wanted Caterina to surrender her rights to "King Zaco's" illegitimate children. Venice reacted in the nick of time and troops from the Serenissima duly landed on Cyprus, at which point the plotters took flight.

The young Jacques III died of a fever that very same year. Flanked by an administrator and two Venetian patricians, the queen now held a purely representative office, and in 1487 the senate decided to annex the kingdom of Cyprus to the dominions of Venice, thus obliging Caterina to renounce the crown. In exchange, she was given the seigniory of Asolo. Here she held sway for twenty years, surrounded by a small court that was refined and elegant, and enlivened by artists and men of letters. As queen of the salon and high society, and a friend of Isabella d'Este and Beatrice Sforza, Caterina Corner inspired many writers and poets. She often returned to Venice and gave sumptuous receptions in the palace on the Grand Canal. She died in her residence on the Grand Canal in 1510, and the palace passed on to her brother Giorgio.

In the eighteenth century, the Corner brothers decided to rebuild their residence in the style of that period. Domenico Rossi was charged with the task, and work on the building continued from 1724 to 1728. The interior also was redesigned with great opulence, doing away with the earlier frescos, which Giambattista Tiepolo had helped to paint. The palace remained in the hands of the Corner family until 1800. The last descendant, Caterina, bequeathed it to the Holy See, but Pope Pius VII gave it as a gift to Antonangelo and Marc' Antonio Cavanis, two priests who had founded a congregation dedicated to the education of young people from the less privileged classes. Then the city of Venice purchased it from the Cavanis brothers and turned it into the offices of a pawnbroking organization, the Monte di Pietà.

At the present time it belongs to the Venice Biennale, which, after various restoration plans, has installed the Historical Archives of Contemporary Art in the building. These archives include a well-endowed library, a newspaper and periodical library, and a photographic library with reproductions of almost all the works that have been shown at the Biennale from 1895 onward.

Antonio Vassillacchi, known as Aliense,
The Arrival of the Queen of Cyprus, Caterina Corner, in Venice.

19 - Palazzo Corner Loredan Piscopia

This palace was built in the Venetian Byzantine style in the thirteenth century for the Boccasi family, originally from Parma. The Boaccasi family died out in the fifteenth century. Ownership of the building subsequently passed to the Ziani family, whose most celebrated scion was the doge Sebastiano Ziani, who, in Venice in 1177, brokered the peace between Pope Alexander III and Frederick Barbarossa.

In the fourteenth century, Federico Corner, the wealthiest man of the day in the Serenissima, purchased the palace. He ran commercial and industrial businesses and had interests here, there, and everywhere in the Near East. In 1366 together with his brothers, he made a colossal loan to Pierre II of Lusignan, king of Cyprus, who was then under threat from the Turks. Federico played host to the monarch in his palace on the Grand Canal and obtained from him the appointment to fief of Piscopia in Cyprus, with concessions to cultivate and refine sugar there, exempt from duty and taxes. What is more, King Pierre also dubbed Federico a knight of the Order of the Sword, which explains the still visible allegorical and heraldic decorations carved on the façade of his residence: David and Goliath, Justice and Might, the royal coat of arms of the Lusignans and the coat of arms of the Corners with the sword of the order set perpendicular, and the words *Pro tuenda integritate*. In 1377 Federico was host to Valentina Visconti, whose hand had been promised to King Pierre II of Cyprus, and in 1389 Francesco Gonzaga, lord of Mantua, stayed in the palace. Above all, however, the palace's past is bound up with stories about Giovanni Battista Corner and his amorous exploits, and about his daughter, Elena Lucrezia, who had a degree in philosophy from the University of Padua. Giovanni Battista, procurator of San Marco, caused a stir when he decided to take as his second wife Zanitta Boni, a woman of

humble origins. She came from the Valsabbia, a remote area under Venetian sway in Lombardy, and she had found her way to Venice "from one brothel to the next," as one of the city's "basest courtesans." After the wedding, she claimed the title of *procuratessa* (procurator) and was extremely jealous of her rank. Nevertheless not a single lady from Venice's high society sought her company, and the *avogadori di Comun* (the city advocates), who were custodians of the Golden Book of the patriarchate, refused pointblank to register the marriage. As a result, her sons Francesco and Girolamo were barred from the Consiglio Maggiore and hence from the patriarchate. It was not until 1664, after their fourth application, sweetened with an offer of one hundred and fifty thousand ducats, that they were admitted.

On a different note, Elena Lucrezia, daughter of Giovanni Battista, was born in 1646. It was her tutor, the priest Giambattista Fabris, who urged her father to let her pursue classical studies. She was entrusted to the care of the "keeper" of the Biblioteca Marciana (Saint Mark's Library), Alvise Ambrogio Gradenigo, a scholar of wide renown, who taught her Latin, Greek, French, Spanish, mathematics, and music. The mathematician Carlo Rinaldini was staggered by Elena's perfect grasp of dialectics, philosophy, theology, and even astrology. She conversed in Hebrew with the rabbis in the ghetto, and at the age of thirty-one she held a solemn philosophical disputation in Latin and Greek before an extremely select audience. Her doctoral dissertation was discussed in the Padua cathedral on 25 June 1678. This was the first time in recorded history that a woman obtained the title of Doctor. She then opted for the life of an ascetic and died in the Corner family palace in Padua at the age of thirty-eight.

In 1703 the palace passed into the hands of the Loredan family, until the early nineteenth century when it was sold and converted into a hotel. In 1864 it was purchased by the city of Venice, and today it is the seat of the Venetian city hall.

20 - Palazzo Corner Mocenigo

In 1535 this residence of the Corners at San Polo was destroyed by fire, just like the Palazzo Corner della Ca' Grande three years earlier.

The Corners entrusted the task of rebuilding the palace to the architect of the Venetian government, Michele Sanmicheli of Verona. On his death in 1560, there was still work to be done, but the building was finally completed in 1564. Vasari describes the San Polo building as "magnificent and most opulent," and Sansovino, as having "a wealth of various decorations."

The already existing fourteenth-century edifice had been given by the Republic first to Giacomo da Carrara in 1349, then to General Gerolamo dal Verme, next to Erasmo da Narni, commonly known as the Gattamelata, and lastly to Francesco Sforza in 1454. Sforza preferred to exchange the San Polo building for the Ca' del Duca in San Samuele, which also belonged to the Corners.

After being owned by the Mocenigo family, the palace is nowadays the headquarters of the Customs and Excise Services.

21 - Palazzo Corner Spinelli

This palace was built between the late fifteenth century and the early sixteenth century by the architect Mauro Codussi. It is a typical early Venetian Renaissance building, in which late Gothic features, such as the traditional division into three parts and three floors, combine with aspects of the Renaissance vocabulary of Florence, for example the use of flat rustication work for the base. Originally designed for the Lando family, the building was subsequently bought in 1540 or thereabouts by Senator Giovanni Corner, grandson of Caterina, queen of Cyprus. Giovanni was eager to alter the interior of the palace to suit his own taste. The task went to Michele Sanmicheli, who remodelled the entrance hall, turning it into a Roman atrium with Tuscan columns and pilasters. He also added a *serliana* that opened on to the garden and a courtyard. The services of Giorgio Vasari were called upon for the decorations. Today, at Palazzo Corner Spinelli nothing remains of Vasari's magnificent ceiling with its famous foreshortened figures. The individual ceiling panels have been scattered throughout various collections; which is rather unfortunate, considering the abiding influence that this work had upon Venetian artists, in particular Paolo Veronese and Jacopo Tintoretto.

In 1740 the residence passed from the heirs of Giovanni Corner to the Spinellis, an extremely wealthy family of silk merchants from Castelfranco, and later to the famous dancer Maria Taglioni, who also owned the Palazzo Busenello and the Palazzo Giustinian Lolin. There were several more changes in ownership – we should mention the English major Edward Cheney, friend of John and Effie Ruskin – before the palace was purchased by the Salom family, to whom it currently belongs.

22 - Palazzo Correr Contarini Zorzi

This handsome eighteenth-century palace is known as the Ca'
dei Cuori (the Dwelling of the Hearts) because of the shape of
the wrought iron coats of arms on the two doorways.

It was here, on 7 January 1758, that Antonio Correr died. He
was the last of the patricians who refused to wear a periwig.
Nowadays this might well seem a trivial and ridiculous matter,
but in those times it was a significant subject of debate. In his
Storia delle leggi e dei costumi dei Veneziani, Giovanni Rossi de-
votes many pages to the topic and from them, we learn that
anyone who did not wear a wig was thought to be a frivolous
and unreliable person.

One of the most illustrious members of this old Venetian family was Angelo Correr. After a term as bishop of Venice, and then
patriarch of Constantinople, he was elected pope in 1406 with
the name of Gregory XII. Shortly after his election, however, he
resigned and went back to being a mere cardinal.

23 - Palazzo d'Anna Viaro Martinengo Volpi di Misurata

Legend has it that even Michelangelo journeyed to Venice to admire the frescos that Pordenone had painted in the first half of the sixteenth century on the façade of the palace belonging to Martino d'Anna. The work, according to Vasari, thoroughly delighted the whole city of Venice, and it was for this that Pordenone received more praise than any other man who had ever worked in that city up until then. We can get some idea of the decoration from a sketch in the Victoria and Albert Museum in London, by an unknown artist: above the door the artist depicted the rape of Proserpine, between the lower side windows, the rape of the Sabine women and Marcus Curtius before the chasm, and on the main floor, Mercury in flight and Cybele in the winged chariot. These frescos had started to become seriously damaged as early as in the seventeenth century, and in the eighteenth century, all that remained was a shadowy figure of Curtius.

The palace was originally built for the Talenti family of Florence, and then almost immediately after it was completed, it was purchased by the Flemish merchant Martino d'Anna, who, according to popular tradition, had stood as godfather to Titian.

After the d'Anna family, the residence was owned by the Viaro family, then the Foscarinis, and lastly the Martinengos.

In the nineteenth century, it was converted first into an asylum and then into the offices of the Banco di Napoli, before being purchased by Count Giuseppe Volpi di Misurata in the early twentieth century. As a conspicuous figure in the Italian industrial and political worlds, it was he who created Porto Marghera and Mestre, which are today much criticized as environmental disaster areas. He had been governor of Libya and during the Fascist period in Italy, was appointed Chancellor of the Exchequer. He died in 1947 at the age of seventy, in Rome, a long way from his palace on the Grand Canal.

24 - Ca' d'Oro

During the period of the Republic, the Palazzo Ducale or Doges' Palace was the only edifice allowed to use the title of palace. The patricians called their residences Casa or Ca', followed by their family name. So does the Ca' d'Oro palace owe its name to the Oro family? No, it does not. Oddly enough, this name comes from the magnificent gilt-work that decorates the façade.

Ca' d'Oro was built in the flamboyant Gothic style between 1422 and 1440 for the public prosecutor Marino Contarini who, in 1412, had bought a property upon which stood a Venetian Byzantine building. And it was in 1431 that he signed a contract with the French painter Jean Charlier, known as Zuane da Franza, to add the splendour of gold to the multi-colored marble. The stones of the crenellations, the sculpted lions on the corner capitals, and the decorations at the top of the curved window arches – all were covered with gold.

Ca' d'Oro passed from proprietor to proprietor until it was finally bought in the nineteenth century by the Russian prince Alexander Trubetskoy, who gave it as a gift to the most acclaimed star of the day, the sublime Maria Taglioni (1804-1884). It would seem that Trubetskoy presented her with the Ca' d'Oro to thank her for having saved him from being banished to Siberia as a liberal, a sentence handed down by Czar Nicholas I, an otherwise fierce, unflinching despot, but one unable to resist the charms of Maria Taglioni.

At that time, the building was in a lamentable state of repair, and according to a surveyor's expert report of the time, the balconies had lost their vaults and windows, and rain poured in through the cracks. One must note however that this famous dancer, whom even Count Radetzky, supreme commander of the Austrian army in Italy, would unhesitatingly call on during his stays in Venice, was a collector of historic edifices on the

Grand Canal. She thus owned the Palazzo Busenello at Sant'Aponal, the Palazzo Giustinian-Lolin by Longhena at San Samuele, and the elegant Palazzo Corner-Spinelli by Codussi at Sant'Angelo. She was intent on having the Ca' d'Oro restored, and accordingly called upon the services of an unscrupulous engineer by the name of Giovanni Battista Meduna. Before the horrified eyes of John Ruskin, who referred to it in his book *The Stones of Venice* (1851-53), Meduna then proceeded to dismantle the floors, break up the pillars and frames, remove the marble, the stones and the capitals – and before very long this plunder earned him a summons to appear in court.

Ca' d'Oro was purchased in 1894 by the musician and collector Giorgio Franchetti, who undertook the restoration of the palace before donating it to the city of Venice. The ashes of Baron Franchetti are kept in the drum of a porphyry column in the courtyard, where we also find the famous red marble well parapet by Bartolomeo Bon, built between 1427 and 1428 – the "great reddish well," as Gabriele d'Annunzio called it.

The palace has been open to the public since 1927. Today it houses a large collection of paintings and art objects, including Andrea Mantegna's *San Sebastiano*, works by Pisanello, Gentile Bellini, and Vittore Carpaccio, and in particular, the remains of the decorative fresco painted in 1508 by Giorgione and Titian on the façade of the Fondaco dei Tedeschi.

25 - Ca' da Mosto

The past of this "simple, elegant, and thrusting" palace – "the most original and perfect," as John Ruskin described it – is mainly associated with Alvise da Mosto, a famous navigator and explorer, born in 1432. At the age of twenty-two, he set sail aboard a merchantman captained by Marco Zeno. At Cape Saint Vincent, he encountered Prince Henry of Portugal, who invited him to take command of a Portuguese caravel. With this ship, Alvise forced a passage along the western shores of Africa, explored Senegal and the Canary Islands and later on, together with Antoniotto Usodimare of Genoa, reached the mouth of the river Gambia and discovered the Cape Verde Islands. After a seven-year stretch spent as a merchant in Lagos, Africa, he returned to Venice where he married Elisabetta Venier. It is likely that he passed away in this palace in 1488.

The construction of this Venetian Byzantine building dates back to the thirteenth century, while the top two floors were added respectively in the seventeenth and eighteenth centuries. Ownership by the da Mosto family is not irrefutably documented until the fifteenth century. The family died out in the early seventeenth century, and the palace was then divided among several proprietors and leased to Zuanne Giarin, who set up the Leon Bianco hotel in the premises. This hotel played host to numerous illustrious visitors to the city. In the latter half of the eighteenth century, Joseph II, Holy Roman Emperor, stayed there on two occasions, and in 1782 Grand Duke Paul Petrovic, son of Catherine II and heir to the imperial Russian throne, stayed there with his wife Maria Feodorovna.

Following the fall of the Republic in 1797, the history of the palace was so shrouded in mystery that the original name for it, "Leon Bianco," was not unearthed until the mid-nineteenth century.

26 - Palazzo Dandolo

"Venus is the beautiful goddess, Venice is the beautiful city. Sweet star, enchanting city, / Pearls of love and beauty, / You lay in the bitter waters, / In the evening, when in your cradles; / For you are sisters, and for mother / You had the spindrift of the waves." The verses penned by George Sand in her Venetian novel, *L'Uscope*, still resound in the rooms of this palace.

For it was precisely here, in the Danieli hotel on the Riva dei Schiavoni, that she and the Romantic poet Alfred de Musset lived some of the moments of their love affair, which started in Paris in 1833. Marcel Proust, too, spent the first of his two long-awaited and much-dreamt-of Venetian visits at the Danieli, whose walls also accommodated Honoré de Balzac and Percy Bysshe Shelley. Built for the Dandolo family at the end of the fourteenth century, the palace then passed to the Mocenigos, whose coats of arms still adorn all the rooms, and then to the Bernardo family. After changing hands several more times, it was then purchased lock, stock, and barrel by Giuseppe dal Niel, otherwise known as Danieli, in the first half of the nineteenth century. He subsequently turned the palace into one of the city's most prestigious hotels, whose guest list included King William of Prussia, the queen of Greece and Queen Isabella of the Two Sicilies. The most recent wing of the hotel, called the Danielino, came into being some fifty years ago on a site whereupon, as a commemorative gesture to the doge Vitale Michiel II who was murdered there in 1172, construction had been prohibited for centuries.

27 - Ca' Dario

In the fifteenth century, Giovanni Dario was one of the few people, not belonging to the Venetian aristocracy, to own a palace on the Grand Canal. His status was that of secretary of state.

In 1479 the Serenissima had entrusted him with the important mission of negotiating peace with Mahomet II, emperor of the Ottoman Turks. Venice had been at war with the Turks for sixteen years and it was high time to put an end to this conflict. Giovanni Dario managed to ratify a treaty which satisfied both Venice, despite the serious losses it incurred (the Republic had to give up Negroponte, Argolis, the Sporades, and the island of Lemnos, and pay the sultan a tribute of ten thousand gold ducats a year in order to be able to trade freely in the Black Sea), and Mahomet II. The sultan presented Dario with three suits interwoven with gold as a gift, and the Serenissima rewarded him with a sizeable sum of money and property at Noventa Padovana. Giovanni fully merited these gifts not only for the successfully accomplished diplomatic mission, but also on account of the cultural exchange that he introduced. It was he who saw to it that Mahomet II invite the painter Gentile Bellini to his court in Istanbul to paint his portrait. A version of this portrait is currently in the National Gallery in London.

With the money he received from the Republic, Giovanni bought a Gothic building on the Grand Canal, to which he added a new façade. This work began in 1487 and the architect may have been Pietro Lombardo. On the narrow façade with its wealth of colored stones, refined decorations mingled with Renaissance arches and classical mouldings. During the initial phase of the work, the owner had a marble inscription built into the lower floor which read *Urbis Genio Joannes Darius* (Giovanni Dario to the Genius of the City). This was restored by John Ruskin in the first half of the nineteenth century.

In 1484 the governor of Venice decided once again to send the now seventy-year-old Giovanni Dario to negotiate with the Turks, but this time with the son of Mahomet II, Bayezid II. To convey their satisfaction with the outcome, the Senate appointed him secretary of the Council of Ten and in addition, provided his daughter Marietta with her dowry.

After Giovanni's death, the palace passed on to his daughter, who had married Vincenzo Barbaro, and it remained in the hands of the age-old patrician family of the Barbaros until the early nineteenth century. Between 1838 and 1842 it belonged to Rawdon Lubbock Brown, a friend of Ruskin, who had purchased the building from the marquis of Abdoll, an Armenian diamond merchant. Rawdon had come to Venice at the age of twenty-seven and never set foot outside the city again. He was a palaeographer, whose project was to transcribe all the documents concerning the history of England in the State Archives of the Serenissima. He also published important research about the sixteenth-century diarist Marin Sanudo.

Once he had restored the palace, he sold it to Count Sigismund Zichy, brother of Princess Metternich. In the years that ensued, thanks to the new proprietor Countess de la Baume, Ca' Dario earned fame for its salon, which was frequented mainly by French men of letters, headed by Henri de Régnier. Others who attended included Edmond Jaloux, Jean-Louis Vaudoyer, Henri Gonse, and Abel Bonnard.

After various changes in ownership and a tragedy involving stormy passions that concluded a homosexual affair, which earned the palace a sinister reputation, Ca' Dario was bought by the Gardini family, in whose hands it has remained. This family came sadly into the limelight some years back, when Raul Gardini, an industrialist mixed up in the so-called Tangentopoli scandal of bribery and corruption in high places, took his own life.

28 - Palazzo Dolfin Manin

The Dolfin family attributes the origin of their name to a figure who was nicknamed Dolfin because of his extraordinary talent as a swimmer. Among their forbears, the Dolfins laid claim to a bishop of Aquileia from as early as 434, a doge, five cardinals, and a smattering of functionaries working for the Republic. The more lighthearted side of the family history involves their patronage of a "company of the stocking," known as the Accesi (Firebrands). The "companies of the stocking" were clubs of young noblemen who amused themselves by mounting various entertainments, pranks, and theatrical shows. They and their valets wore multicoloured stockings which indicated the company to which they belonged. In 1565 Andrea Palladio was given the job of building a wooden theatre for the courtyard of the Palazzo Dolfin. The palace was built for Giovanni Dolfin by Jacopo Sansovino between 1538 and 1574. It remained in the hands of the Dolfin family until 1602, when the family died out and the residence was divided up among the various heirs.

In 1789 Lodovico Manin, the last doge of the Serenissima, acquired the palace and gave the go-ahead for a certain amount of modernization to be undertaken, a task for which Antonio Selva was responsible. The abdication of Lodovico Manin marked the end of the tradition of the doges, and for this reason he was frequently slandered. But it was Napoleon, himself, who exonerated Doge Manin, and in so doing, he pointed the finger at the true culprit, the ambassador Francesco Pesaro – it was the ambassador who had accepted Napoleon's offer to strike up an alliance against the Austrians, and had thus enabled the Republic to be saved; but only temporarily.

Manin's heirs continued to live at San Salvador until 1867. The building subsequently became the offices of the Banca d'Italia.

29 - Palazzo Duodo

Here, on 11 January 1801, the famous composer Domenico Cimarosa passed away while he was putting the finishing touches to his last score *Artemisia di Venezia*. The Palazzo Duodo dates back to the end of the fifteenth century. It remained in the hands of the Duodo family until 1808, when it passed to the Balbi-Venier family, as a result of the marriage of Elisabetta Duodo to Marco Bertucci Balbi-Venier.

30 - Palazzo Falier Canossa

The miraculous discovery of the body of Saint Mark in 1094 (depicted by Tintoretto in one of his canvases) occurred, as it happens, during the dogeship of Vitale, an illustrious forbear of the Faliers. The family palace was built in the first half of the fifteenth century – the two projecting wings with loggias were added at a later date – and remained the residence of the Falier family until they died out in this present century. In 1492 the proprietor was Francesco Falier who, in that same year, was banished for life to the island of Cyprus. He had in fact suggested to the Council of Ten that one hundred ducats a year should be donated to those patricians most in need, and according to the calculations made by the council, the sum to be put aside for this purpose would have amounted to seventy thousand ducats, a figure deemed to be ruinous. Out of 1,800 patricians, some 1,225 were in fact eligible to receive such a grant. For all this, Francesco soon made good his return to Venice and became head of the Council of Ten. In a quite different vein, Francesco's father, Giovanni, can be credited with having initiated the studies of Antonio Canova. It appears that the young Canova was employed as a kitchen-boy in the Falier villa at Pradazzi di Asolo, and that one day, when Giovanni saw the lad modelling a lion out of butter, he decided to dispatch him to Venice. There is no doubt that Canova made the group of *Daedalus and Icarus*, which is now in the Correr Museum, for Giovanni Falier.

In the 1860s one of the apartments situated on the mezzanine of the building was rented to a young American writer, William Dean Howells, who had been sent by Abraham Lincoln to Venice as an American consul. Howells remained there until 1865, and subsequently published his book *Venetian Life*, a veritable bestseller in its time. To this day, a notice on the side of the palace facing Calle Vitturi records Howells' period of residence.

31 - Ca' Farsetti

According to the chronicler Stefano Magno, following the conquest of Constantinople in 1204, Doge Enrico Dandolo sent some marble to Venice and ordered his son to use it to build a palace. This tale is nevertheless contradicted by another Dandolo doge, Andrea, who in referring to Ca' Farsetti, which he had purchased, said that "it was not far" from Enrico's. Andrea, who was a friend of Petrarch, was a humanist, historian, and jurist, and he was in contact with the most important scholars in Europe.

On 3 December 1524 the palace came close to being totally destroyed by a terrible fire. Luckily, the roof collapsed, smothering the flames. After this close shave, Marino Dandolo had the main façade rebuilt so that it gives on to the Grand Canal instead of the Campiello della Chiesa.

In the mid-seventeenth century, the residence passed into the hands of Anton Francesco Farsetti. The Farsetti family, from Tuscany, was a highly cultured one, and they were enthusiastic collectors and patrons of the arts. Abbot Filippo Vincenzo collected models and plaster casts of the most famous ancient sculptures (today in the Gallerie dell'Accademia) and made them available to young artists. Furthermore, he even paid a sculptor to assist the most deserving beginners. One such young artist was Antonio Canova. Before they were moved to the City Museum (Museo Civico), two marble fruit-filled baskets could be seen beside the grand staircase of the palace – Canova's early work.

The last of the Farsettis, Anton Francesco, squandered the entire family fortune. After the fall of the Republic, he sold the paintings in the gallery, and gave the statues to Czar Paul I when he moved to Saint Petersburg in search of fortune. He died there in 1808. For some years afterward, the palace was used as a hotel, until it was bought by the city of Venice in 1826, and turned into the municipal offices.

32 - Fondaco dei Turchi

It was a certain Giacomo Palmieri, erstwhile consul of Pesaro and member of a noble family of merchants, who had this palace constructed in the thirteenth century in the Venetian Byzantine style. Today it is known as the Fondaco dei Turchi. It seems that it was designed expressly to allow large galleys to berth and unload merchandise, such as sacks of ginger and pepper, bales of Chinese silk, and cloth from England.

In 1381 it was acquired by the Republic, which then gave it as a gift to the marquis of Ferrara, Nicolò d'Este, for the loyalty he had shown during the Naval War of Chioggia. And from that time on, the palace became the "floating" property of the Este family: whenever their relations with the Serenissima soured, the Serenissima would confiscate it, only to restore it to them when the relationship improved once more. This is what happened in 1483, when Ferrara was at loggerheads with Venice over the latter's attempts to expand inland, and again in 1509, the year in which the Estes joined the anti-Venetian League of Cambrai.

The Republic also used the building to accommodate the more illustrious foreign visitors to the city and their retinues. For the Council of Ferrara, convened in February 1438, John VIII Paleologus, emperor of Byzantium, arrived by sea, together with the patriarch of Constantinople. The imperial fleet, escorted by Venetian ships and proceeding into the eastern Mediterranean from one Venetian port to the next, took more than two months to reach Venice. The emperor was accompanied by more than 650 orthodox ecclesiastes.

The palace also housed Pandolfo Malatesta, Dom Pedro of Portugal (who toured the city with trumpeters and fife players to entice the women out onto their balconies), the king of Dacia, Emperor Frederick III of Hapsburg, René of Anjou, and Bona Sforza, queen of Poland.

Turks did not take up residence here until the early years of the seventeenth century, when the new owner, Doge Antonio Priuli, decided to lease it to some Turkish merchants. For some time already, the Seigniory had the idea of bringing together, under one roof, as it were, merchants, businessmen, and middlemen, hailing not only from Turkey, but from all the regions under the sway of the sovereign of Constantinople. Doors and windows were closed in accordance with the Moslem custom, and a mosque was installed, as were baths. However, the fact that admission to the palace was forbidden, by the Republic, to beardless young Christian men and to Christian women attests to the diehard prejudices then fostered against the Turks.

With the decline of trade with the Orient, the number of merchants started to drop off and the income from the leasehold diminished as a result. The state of the building deteriorated more and more, until there was a major collapse in 1732. Yet, Turks continued to reside in it until 1838. The last of them, a certain Saddo-Drisdi, was forced to leave by the Manin family, which had inherited the palace from the Pesaros.

It has been the property of the city since 1860, who restored it in 1869, and today it houses the Museum of Natural History.

33 - Palazzo Fortuny

When you venture into the small Campo di San Beneto, the impressive Gothic façade of this late-fifteenth-century palace rises before your eyes. It was built for the Pesaro family, which some genealogists say is descended directly from Jupiter.

In the early sixteenth century, the building was often the scene of theatrical performances, as in February 1515, when young noblemen belonging to a "company of the stocking" recited Plautus' *Miles Gloriosus* in the main courtyard. Among the audience at the recital were the children of Doge Leonardo Loredan and the ambassador of the king of France. The show was followed by a supper and a ball, in which revellers danced until dawn. When, in the eighteenth century, the Pesaros moved to the new family residence on the Grand Canal, the residence of San Beneto became the seat of the Accademia filarmonica degli Orfei, which organized balls and concerts here. Subsequently, the palace was purchased by the Accademia Apollinea, which would later move to the premises of La Fenice.

In the early years of this century, ownership of the palace passed on to Mariano Fortuny y Madrazo, a Spanish painter, set designer, collector, and friend of Proust and d'Annunzio. Mariano rediscovered the dyes used by sixteenth-century dyers and the processes whereby Venetians wove fabrics with gold and silver thread. With his own priceless fabrics, he dressed Eleonora Duse, Sarah Bernhardt, and the dancer Isadora Duncan. He also developed a series of inventions related to stage direction and set design.

The artist's widow handed the palace over to the city of Venice in 1956, to be used for cultural activities, shows, and exhibitions. At the present time it houses the Fortuny Museum, the Virgilio Guidi Donation, and the Center of Photographic Documentation.

34 - Palazzo Foscari

The Giustinian family had this palace built towards the end of the fourteenth century, and in 1420 the Republic purchased it for 6,500 ducats. The Council of Ten decided to give it as a gift to the marquis of Mantua, Gian Francesco Gonzaga but, just ten years later, it duly confiscated the palace from the marquis when he struck up an alliance with the duke of Milan. The palace then passed into the hands of Count Francesco Sforza. In due course, the Serenissima put the palace up for auction and it was bought by Francesco Foscari, doge of Venice from 1423 to 1457.

Francesco Foscari spent his boyhood in Egypt, where his father had been exiled for reasons that are still mysterious. By the age of twenty-seven, he had become a senator, by thirty-one, an *avogador* or magistrate, and at the tender age of fourty-four, procurator of San Marco. Four years later he was elected doge, which made him the youngest doge in the history of Venice. During his dogeship, the Venetians extended their sway as far as the banks of the river Adda in Lombardy, as a result of the ten-year war against the Viscontis of Milan.

It was in the year 1440 that Francesco's son, Jacopo, married Lucrezia Contarini. On the night of the wedding, the doge personally led the bride and her 150 attendant ladies on his sumptuous Bucentaur, from San Barnaba to the Doge's Palace, where an evening banquet was served. A retinue of ladies and knights crossed a bridge made of boats spanning the water between San Samuele and San Barnaba to go and fetch the bride. In Piazza San Marco, there was a tournament with jousting, in which no lesser figures than the marquis of Ferrara, the marquis of Monferrato, and the son of Francesco Sforza all took part. For some years nothing was heard about Jacopo's life, but in 1445 a scandal erupted. Rumour reached the Council of Ten that the doge's son had accepted valuable gifts in exchange of bestowing improper favours on certain transactions and persons. He was ordered to be arrested and was subsequently exiled to Nauplia in Rumania, though this banishment was duly commuted to forced residence in Treviso. At his father's request, he was recalled two years later. But on the night of 5 November 1450, a patrician was killed while returning home. Because he had been a member of the Council of Ten when the verdict against Jacopo had been pronounced, and because a servant of Jacopo had been seen close to the Doge's Palace at the time of the murder, the doge's son was once again arrested and exiled, this time, to the island of Crete. Jacopo was in fact innocent, but by the time Nicolò Erizzo confessed to the murder on his deathbed, Jacopo had already passed away. It was from these tragic events that Lord Byron drew the subject of the tragedy *The Two Foscari*, which was later adapted for Verdi's libretto of the same title.

Francesco Foscari was then eighty-four years old and incapable of executing his own duties as doge, so the Council of Ten forced him to resign. He died just a few days later – and, if we are to believe the legend   at the very moment when the bells announced the election of the new doge, Pasquale Malipiero.

Nevertheless this palace evokes memories other than sad ones. It played host to various illustrious guests at feasts and regattas on the Grand Canal, including Ferdinand and Maximilian of Austria in 1579, Ernst, duke of Brunswick in 1686, and King Ferdinand IV of Denmark in 1709.

In 1574 it was chosen by Henri III of Valois, king of France and Poland, as his residence during his state visit; he was accommodated, as it happens, in a room beside the one in which Francesco Foscari died. The king and his spouse, Eleonora of France, were received at Murano by the doge, attended by sixty *halbardiers* clad in silk and forty young patricians. On board the Bucentaur, they made their way to Ca' Foscari, which had been draped with imprinted and gilded leather, rare fabrics, and ancient weaponry.

In a kind of loggia built on large vessels, an orchestra played highly refined pieces of music. A floating glass furnace worked all night long in front of the palace, lighting up the Grand Canal with reflections from fire and glass paste glowing red hot. The plates, settings, and decorations for the banqueting table were all designed by Sansovino and made of sugar. A regatta was organized and today the floating stand for the various dignitaries is still moored alongside the Ca' Foscari.

During the period of Austrian rule, the palace was requisitioned by the military authorities and turned into barracks. In 1847 it was purchased by the city, which painstakingly restored it and then used it for the University Institute of Economics and Commerce. Today it is the main seat of the University of Venice.

35 - Palazzo Giustinian

Certain people hold that the origins of the Giustinian family date back to the ancient Roman *gens* or clan of the Anici, while others consider Justinian the Great and his nephew and son-in-law Justin, emperor of the Eastern Empire, to be the progenitors of the family. In 670 Justin's son, Justinian, left Constantinople for Istria, where he lent his name to the city of Justinopolis, present-day Capodistria. From here, his descendants moved first to Malamocco, on the Lido, and subsequently to Venice where they were admitted to the Council of Ten. According to popular tradition, the family almost died out in the twelfth century because all the male offspring had died in a battle against the Byzantine emperor, Manuel Eroticus Comnenus. The sole survivor was a youthful Justinian, but he had taken religious vows and was a monk at San Niccolò del Lido. Well aware of the importance and worth of the Giustinian family, the members of the grand Morosini and Falier families made an appeal to Pope Alexander III, requesting that the young scion's vows be annulled and that he be permitted to marry. So it was that Niccolò Giustinian ended up marrying Anna, daughter of Doge Vitale Falier II, with all due solemnity. The couple bore nine sons and three daughters. Having saved the family from extinction, Niccolò withdrew and practiced a meditative life of contemplation, and his wife followed his example, taking the veil at the convent of Sant'Adriano di Costanziaca, which she herself founded. The last descendant of the Giustinian family died in Venice in 1962.

Work on the palace probably got under way in about 1452 and in reports of the day, there was mention of no less than three palaces, one of which was sold by the Giustinians to the Foscaris, who had it pulled down. Bartolomeo Bon, the architect responsible for the two buildings, which together, form the Palazzo Giustinian, designed two quite separate palaces, which were

nevertheless joined together, both externally and from within. Two branches of the family, the Giustinian dei Vescovis and the Giustinian dalle Zogies, resided in these palaces.

After the fall of the Republic in 1797, the old Gothic edifice was acquired by the painter Natale Schiavone, who installed an important collection of artworks in its rooms.

One of the most famous guests at the palace was Richard Wagner, who on his first visit to Venice in 1858, chose it as his residence for a seven-month sojourn. He was fond of wandering round the vast and majestic rooms, in which the piano had a wonderful sound. He draped the rooms of his apartment in dark red velvet, which is what he also did at the Palazzo Vendramin Calergi. While staying at the Palazzo Giustinian, he composed *Tristan and Isolde*, started work on *Parsifal*, and studied Schopenhauer and the teachings of Buddha. He interrupted his studies every day with a gondola ride to Piazza San Marco (Saint Mark's Square) and to judge from his Venetian journals, he often entertained thoughts of suicide.

In the latter half of the nineteenth century, the palace played host to the novelist William Dean Howells, who had been dispatched to Venice as a consul by Abraham Lincoln towards the end of 1861 and stayed there until 1865.

Following double page: small salon of a private apartment in the Palazzo Giustinian, a typical eighteenth-century Venetian interior.

36 - Palazzo Giustinian Lolin

In 1623 when Giovanni Lolin left his palace on the Grand Canal to his nephew Giovanni Giustinian, reconstruction of the edifice was already under way. The modernization of the old fourteenth-century palace was entrusted to the young Baldassare Longhena, who redesigned the façade by adapting it to the Baroque style of the day.

When the Republic fell, the palace was acquired by Francesco Aglietti. This renowned physician and collector of rare books lived in the palace until 1836. Ownership of the residence then passed on to the dancer Maria Taglioni, and later to Duchess Maria Luisa of Parma, who was the daughter of Marie Caroline of Bourbon and the wife of Charles III of Bourbon, duke of Parma, Piacenza, and Guastalla. Luisa spent several months a year in the Palazzo Giustinian Lolin, dividing her time between it and her residence at Wartegg. She died in one of the rooms overlooking the Grand Canal in 1864. Her son, Enrico, count of Bardi, sold the palace to the banker Ugo Levi and moved to the Palazzo Vendramin Calergi.

At the time when Ugo Levi bought the palace, he had started to devote his energies exclusively to culture and the arts. He was an enthusiastic connoisseur of music and a collector of scores, and together with his wife Olga, he held the most musical of Venice's salons. After their concerts, famous soloists were often invited to the Levi home, where they would give an impromptu concert for the guests gathered. The nickname by which Ugo Levi was known in Venice, Ugo Mio Fio (Ugo My Son) came from the undying admiration in which his father held him. Father and son almost always returned home together from Saint Mark's Square – where they had been at the Casino di Commercio, a club for the upper echelons of the bourgeoisie or at the café Florian – with one jacket pocket empty and the other full of beans. Each time one of the two met someone they knew, they moved a bean from one pocket to the other. When they reached the bar "del Gobo" (the bar of the Hunchbacked) in Campo Santo Stefano, they would count the beans, and the one who had greeted fewer people en route and who therefore transferred the fewest beans, picked up the tab for the aperitif.

Olga Levi came from Trieste, and was said to be extremely beautiful, elegant, and sophisticated – everything it took to bestir the admiration of a poet like Gabriele d'Annunzio. The evening after he had first met her, he was there beneath her window in a gondola, escorted by musicians and singers, to dedicate a serenade to her. D'Annunzio became a devoted habitué at the Levi salon, where he would beseech Ugo to perform some music for him on the piano. D'Annunzio was deeply in love with Olga, whom he rechristened with a variety of affectionate pet names, but his favourite of them all was Venturina, after the ever-changing golden hue of her eyes, akin to that of the semiprecious stone that bears this name. Olga, however, treated him like a friend, with familiarity and affability. A rich exchange of letters attests to their friendship.

Today the palace houses the Ugo and Olga Levi Foundation, a center for musical studies and owner of the important music library left behind by Ugo.

37 - Palazzo Giustinian Morosini

This palace, built in approximately 1474 for the Giustinian family and subsequently owned by the Morosinis, is known above all for having been the famous Hôtel de l'Europe during the nineteenth century. Its guests included Chateaubriand, Stendhal, George Eliot, and Marcel Proust. At the present time it houses city offices and the offices of the Biennale.

38 - Palazzo Grassi

The Palazzo Grassi, an elegant building in the classical style, was designed by Giorgio Massari from 1749 on and completed after his death. The Grassi family originally came from Bologna, and had been admitted to the Venetian patriarchate between 1810 and 1820. The palace on the Grand Canal was built for Angelo Grassi, who had carved on the staircase the motto *Concordia res parvae crescunt, discordia etiam maximae dilabuntur* (With concord small things grow, with discord even the greatest things fall into ruin). In his *Memorie di casi avvenuti a Venezia*, the priest Carlo Zilli relates how Giovanni Grassi, in obedience to paternal admonition, accepted the extremely numerous intrigues and love affairs of his wife Margherita Condulmer – to such a degree that, when his wife was abandoned by her gallant and devoted admirer Baccalario Zen, it was Giovanni himself who implored him to make amends with her. With such an obliging and understanding husband, the noblewoman certainly never had to resort to using the many secret staircases in the palace, which had been included in the design by the architect Massari "to hide mysterious love affairs," as a nineteenth-century guide to the city puts it.

The Grassi family died out in the first half of the nineteenth century, and the heirs of the palace were the counts Tornielli. Later, after having been the property of the tenor Antonio Poggi, it became a hotel. It was then the headquarters of the Stabilimento per Bagni (the Bathing Establishment), initiated by Francesco degli Antoni, who used the water of the Grand Canal for this purpose. After changing hands several more times, it was finally bought in 1983 by the Fiat company, who employed the architects Gae Aulenti and Antonio Foscari to undertake a wholesale restoration and renovation of the building into a center for exhibitions and cultural events.

39 - Palazzo Grimani

Legend has it that a Grimani son fell madly in love with a Tiepolo daughter, who lived almost opposite him in the palace now called the Palazzo Papadopoli. He asked her hand in marriage but his proposal was turned down by her father, who said: "It will never be said that I gave the hand of my daughter to a good-for-nothing who does not even have a palace by the canal." After this insulting riposte, the young Grimani had a palace, with windows that dwarfed the door of the Tiepolo residence, built on the canal. It is said that the foundations were made of a timber so valuable that it was worth more than the rest of the building.

In his book *Venetia nobilissima*, Sansovino deems the Palazzo Grimani to be one of the four most important palaces on the Grand Canal.

Girolamo Grimani, procurator and knight of San Marco, charged the architect Michele Sanmicheli with the project. However, a hypothesis has been put forward that Sanmicheli based his plans on a project originally drawn up by Palladio, from whom the previous proprietors of the land, the Contarini family, had commissioned a preliminary study to appraise the timeliness of an investment or, quite simply, to develop the potential of the property. Work on the palace got under way in 1561 and was not completed until 1575, by which time Sanmicheli was dead.

The façade on the Grand Canal seems ideally suited to sumptuous events, implicitly called to mind through its triumphal arches. In 1576 the palace was host to the dukes of Mantua. A feast was organized in their honour, in which the one hundred fairest noblewomen of the city took part, dressed completely in white "and all bedecked in quantities of gold and jewels," as Sansovino put it.

However the most grandiose feast of all was put on to celebrate the coronation of the dogaressa Morosina Grimani, wife of Doge

The *portego* of the principal floor.

Marino Grimani. On 4 May 1597 the Council of Ten and sixty senators, escorted by secretaries and ducal chancellors, made their way on the Bucentaur to the Palazzo Grimani. There, the official procession climbed the main staircase until it reached the main floor, where it was received by the dogaressa. After thanking "the said Lords for the inconvenience suffered," Morosina Grimani swore the doge's oath – a litany of promises, duties, and obligations – and gave the doge's counsellors and the grand chancellor seven sacks of gold and a medal with her effigy on it. She was then taken by boat to the Doge's Palace, where her arrival marked the start of a whole series of receptions and festivities. The coronation of the doge's wife stirred up such emotion throughout Italy that Pope Clement VIII sent her the Rosa d'Oro (the Golden Rose), which she duly bequeathed to the treasury of the basilica of San Marco. After this offering and after the banquet, there was a "most solemn festival of naval war by the English" in the basin of San Marco and, to the great joy of the Venetian populace, various regattas.

After the fall of the Republic, the building was acquired by the Austrian government, which turned it into the headquarters of the Post Office (I.R. Direzione delle Poste).

When Venice was annexed to the kingdom of Italy, the Palazzo Grimani became the seat of the Court of Appeal, which to this day it remains.

40 - Palazzo Grimani Marcello

This residence was known by the name Grimani dall'Albero d'Oro (Grimani of the Golden Tree). It is believed that the capitals and friezes were painted in gold, so that the bright hues reflected by precious marble carried the luxuriousness of the interior to the exterior of the edifice. It would seem that the ballroom, situated on the main floor, was embellished by Tintoretto with a lavish frieze representing the festival of Bacchus. The sixteenth-century plan – the previous building dated back to the thirteenth century – is attributed to Giovanni Buora, who built it for the Grimani family, descendants, according to legends, of Grimoaldo the Lombard king.

The palace remained in the hands of the Grimanis until the twentieth century, when ownership passed first to Count Marcello Grimani Giustinian, and then to the Sorlini family.

41 - Palazzo Gussoni Cavalli Franchetti

The Cavalli family, originally from Bavaria, bought this late-fifteenth-century Gothic palace from an old patrician family, the Gussonis, in the early years of the sixteenth century. It remained in their ownership until the 1830s, when it was purchased by Archduke Frederick of Austria, son of Archduke Charles who had defeated Napoleon at the battle of Aspern. Sadly, however, the archduke did not manage to enjoy his residence on the Grand Canal: in 1847 he died, at the young age of twenty-seven.

The Palazzo Cavalli then passed into the hands of another figure with royal blood, Henri de Bourbon Artois, duke of Bordeaux and count of Chambord. He was the only living heir of the senior branch of the house of Bourbon, pretender to the throne during the time of the Sun King and Louis XV. At the time Louis-Philippe d'Orléans was ruling in Paris, while Henri, together with his wife Maria Teresa d'Este, daughter of the duke of Modena, were leading a quiet life in Venice. However, it was a life governed by court etiquette. She was said to be ungainly and dull, as well as deaf, but more serious was her inability to bear children. So it was that Henri's last hope of providing an heir for the dynasty was dashed.

In 1850 and 1851 Marie-Thérèse of France, daughter of Louis XVI and Marie-Antoinette, also spent several months in the Salon des Oiseaux and the Red Salon, Henri's favourite rooms.

In 1866 the counts of Chambord moved out and ownership was transferred to Baron Raimondo Franchetti.

The baron carried on the restoration work started by Henri de Chambord, entrusting the project to Camillo Boito, who redesigned the façade as well as the interior of the palace in the neogothic style of the time; he also built the lavish stairway that leads to the garden. At the present time the building is the headquarters of the Mediovenezie Banking Institute.

42 - Palazzo Gussoni Grimani della Vida

This palace was originally constructed in the Venetian Byzantine style, and in the mid-sixteenth century it was rebuilt for the Gussoni family by Michele Sanmicheli. The frescos on the façade, all trace of which has now vanished, were painted by Jacopo Tintoretto. He painted two figures inspired by Michelangelo's *Dawn* and *Dusk* (which were sculpted for the tombs of the Medicis in Florence), as well as the figures of Adam and Eve, and Cain and Abel. The Gussoni family, which came originally from Belluno, had arrived in Venice in the early eleventh century. Among the members of this family there were many knights, senators, and ambassadors in the various courts of Europe. In 1735, with the death of Senator Giulio Gussoni, the sixteenth-century residence passed half into the hands of his wife Faustina Lazari and half into the hands of his daughter Giustiniana.

Giustiniana is remembered mainly for her elopement with Count Francesco Taxis of Bergamo. The story is that on Sunday, 16 December 1731, Giustiniana left the palace unaccompanied, boarded a gondola, and went to meet Count Taxis. When they reached Padua in a post coach, they continued their flight in a one-horse carriage, and managed to get to safety beyond the border of the Venetian Republic. "That very same evening in the presence of the priest and witnesses," their marriage was celebrated, and duly announced to the Council of Ten in numerous letters sent by the count himself. The council, however, refused to believe him and ordered that Taxis be arrested. The count was banished in his absence and Giustiniana returned to Venice.

After changing hands several times, the palace was purchased by Cesare della Vida, a wealthy Jewish businessman, after whom the building is now named. It was later bought by the Ministry of Finance and it is now the headquarters of the regional tax inspectorate.

43 - Palazzo Labia

The Labia family hailed originally from Gerona in Catalonia, where they were called Lasbias, and they had come to Venice in the mid-sixteenth century, by way of Avignon and Florence. They were admitted to the ranks of Venetian patricians in 1646, not least as a result of their disbursement of three hundred thousand ducats to support the War of Candia. Giovan Francesco Labia thus decided to build a palace worthy of his new status, in the Baroque style. For his residence, he chose the sight alongside the old church of San Geremia, just where the Grand Canal and the Rio di Cannaregio meet. Work on the building started in the mid-1660s and was not completed until the second decade of the eighteenth century. In the mid-eighteenth century, moreover, Paolo Antonio Labia, great-grandson of the original builder of the palace, had the edifice enlarged onto Campo San Geremia. It is still debatable who actually built the palace. The names of two architects have come down to us, Alessandro Tremignon and Andrea Cominelli, but it is still not clear which architect built which part and when each of them worked on the palace. One thing is certain however: the history of the building involves two building phases.

The fame of the palace is largely due to the frescos painted by Giambattista Tiepolo in the mid-eighteenth century. In the salon on the main floor, the artist painted the story of Antony and Cleopatra, while in two other rooms he painted the figures of Zephyr and Flora, and Bacchus and Ariadne. Some observers have claimed to recognize the patron Paolo Antonio Labia in the portly figure, with the proud face and bonnet-like hat, who seems to be witnessing the scene of Antony and Cleopatra's landing. Who knows if he was indeed the character who, as legend has it, had the habit of hurling gold crockery out of the window at the end of a banquet, saying wittily, "L'abia o no l'abia, sarò sempre Labia." (Whether I have it or not, I shall always be Labia). The tale is also told that a net was stretched across the waters of the canal and that the treasure was fished out of the deep as soon as the guests had left.

There is no doubt that the Labias were one of the wealthiest families in Venice and the jewelry belonging to Paolo Antonio's mother, Maria Labia Civran, was well-known for its outstanding quality. Even the young French nobleman Charles de Brosses, while travelling in Italy, wrote in his letters that her jewels were "possibly the finest owned by any private individual in Europe." Maria herself, and not just her jewels, was renowned for being one of the most beautiful women of her day. She was so beautiful, indeed, that King Frederick IV of Denmark included her on the list of beautiful women whose portraits he commissioned Rosalba Carriera to paint for him.

In the nineteenth century, the palace was sold by the Labia family, now in decline, to Prince Lobkowitz, who in turn sold it to a Jewish religious foundation. It subsequently became a school and was then converted to low rent apartments, wherein the salon with the Tiepolo frescos was used for drying the laundry. The palace was restored in the 1970s, and after being bought by the oil magnate Carlos de Beistegui, it now houses the RAI, the Italian radio and television company.

Opposite : the main salon of the principal floor,
decorated with frescos by Giambattista Tiepolo.
On the wall, to the right, *The meeting of Antony and Cleopatra*.

44 - Palazzo Loredan degli Ambasciatori

The palace of the Loredan family at San Barnaba was constructed in the late sixteenth century in the Venetian Gothic style. The two statues of horsemen in the niches of the façade however are a contribution from the Lombard school of Antonio Rizzo. The branch of the San Barnaba Loredan family came to the fore mainly through the figure of Antonio Loredan, administrator of Corfu. Together with Count Matthias von der Schulenburg, a Saxon general who had confronted Charles XII in Sweden, Loredan had managed to defeat the Turks in 1716 and thus check their advance towards Venice.

Field marshall von der Schulenburg had accepted a three-year contract with the Serenissima, but he was so fond of Venice that he had it renewed until his death. As a guest of the Loredans, he chose as his residence their palace on the Grand Canal, where he set up home with a retinue of twenty-five people and four gondoliers. His table was host to the most illustrious Venetians and travellers. Doge Carlo Ruzzini paid him incognito visits, wearing a mask, as was *de rigueur* for all the private outings of the Serenissima. He was also a highly enthusiastic collector and enjoyed close friendships with several artists such as Giambattista Piazzetta and Antonio Guardi. When he died, there were at least 845 pictures in his collection, most notably, works by Lorenzo Lotto, Caravaggio, Rubens, and Mantegna.

In 1752 Francesco Loredan was elected doge and he decided to offer his palace as a residence for the ambassador of the Holy Roman Empire, on the condition that a contract be drawn up, indicating that the restoration of the building would be paid for by the embassy, for at least twenty-nine years. The first imperial ambassador to live in the palace, henceforth known as the Palazzo dell'Ambasciatore, was Count Philip Orsini Rosenburg, who is known to us above all for having married, at a late age,

the intriguing and much talked about Giustiniana Wynne. As
the illegitimate daughter of an English gentleman and a very
beautiful Greek woman, Giustiniana's teenage years had been
turbulent and spirited. She fell desperately in love with Andrea
Memmo and their intense passion produced a son, who was
born near Paris, in a monastery to which Giustiniana had fled
to keep her pregnancy secret. In Paris she was received by
Giacomo Casanova who wasted no time whatsoever in consol-
ing the miserable Giustiniana in his arms. After a failed marriage
to an extremely wealthy *fermier général* and many other adventures, she left Paris and went to Brussels and then to London
where, to her great displeasure, she failed to be received at court.
After another disastrous marriage in London, she returned to
Italy and settled in Padua. Here she discovered that Andrea
Memmo was deeply in love with another woman. She ended up
marrying Count Rosenberg, an eccentric widower, who was now
getting on in years. The count died not so very long afterwards
in 1765. Giustiniana went on living in Venice as guest of her
husband's heir, Count Giacomo Durazzo, until she was no longer
able to acquit her gambling debts and she took refuge in Padua,
where she held a salon that was frequented by the intelligentsia
of that city. When she died she was a mere fifty-four years old.
The palace remained in the hands of the Loredan family until
the end of the nineteenth century.

45 - Palazzo Malipiero

Beneath the classical façade built in approximately 1622, there are few surviving traces of the old Palazzo dei Cappello that was built in the Venetian Byzantine style. The modernization of the building was commissioned by Caterino Malipiero and probably entrusted to Longhena.

The Malipieros, who had come to the lagoon from Altino when Venice was in the throes of being founded, provided the Serenissima with two doges, Orio – who after a reign of 14 years, abdicated and became a monk – and Pasquale.

A frequent guest at Ca' Malipiero was Giacomo Casanova; until he was discovered making love with a girl, with whom the elderly senator Alvise Gasparo was madly infatuated. After this episode, Casanova left his birth place, the district of San Samuele, forever.

The Malipiero family died out in 1826, and after various changes of ownership, the palace was purchased by the Balbi family.

The present-day proprietors restored the building and unearthed beams and stuccowork that had vanished under the modernization project carried out during the nineteenth century.

46 - Palazzo Mangilli Valmarana Smith

"He who enters your house finds therein the most perfect marriage of all of the sciences and the arts, and you are seated in the midst of them not as a lover contemplating them but as a connoisseur determined to explain them. Your refined taste and your perfect culture have led you to choose the very best of things." It was with these words that Goldoni described Joseph Smith, the British consul in Venice from 1744-1766, in *The English Philosopher*. His house on the Grand Canal had in effect become a temple of high culture, frequented as much by passing foreigners as by the most illustrious figures of eighteenth-century Venice – such as Carlo Lodoli, Francesco Algarotti, Andrea Memmo, and Scipione Maffei. The Gothic-Byzantine style palace was purchased by Joseph Smith in 1740 and accordingly altered to suit the taste of the day. The old asymmetrical façade was radically transformed, the restoration project being clearly inspired by Palladian design.

Joseph Smith enjoyed the friendship and acuaintance of various artists, and thus the palace housed an outstanding collection of contemporary Italian works of art, which were displayed against an English style décor. He owned works by Canaletto (for example, the fourteen views of the Grand Canal, painted between 1730 and 1735, which are now on view at the Windsor Castle), Marco and Sebastiano Ricci, Rosalba Carriera, and Pietro Longhi. His library included a collection of engraved precious stones, manuscripts of Johann Sebastian Bach, and a magnificent collection of drawings, engravings, and prints, which are now in safekeeping in the Royal Library at Windsor.

The palace left the hands of the Smith family in 1775. It was purchased by Caterina Da Mula-Pisani and then by Count Giuseppe Mangilli in 1784. Two floors were added to the building by Giannantonio Selva and the terrace was converted into a series of bedrooms.

47 - Palazzo Mastelli del Cammello

The Palazzo Mastelli del Cammello is so-named on account of the relief on the façade depicting a man pulling along a camel behind him. This was the insignia of the Mastelli family, who sold spices here in Cannaregio. They belonged to the wealthy merchant bourgeoisie and were admitted to the Consiglio Maggiore. However, they were later barred from the council, for reasons still unknown today. Legend has it that the statues built into the side of the palace were portraits of the three brothers, Rioba, Sandi, and Alfani – the heads of the Mastelli family, who arrived in Venice in 1112 from Morea, as the Peloponnese was then known. Because of their southerly origins, they were called the Moors, and Campo dei Mori is named after these carved figures. The corner statue, to which, in the nineteenth century, a large metal nose was affixed, is called Sior Antonio Rioba and it is the model for a character associated with hoaxes and satire.

48 - Palazzo Memmo Martinengo

For many years afterward, there was still talk in Venice about the sumptuous reception given in the Palazzo Memmo at San Marcuola (San Marcuola is the abbreviated Venetian dialect form combining the saints Ermagora and Fortunato) on the occasion of the election of Andrea Memmo as procurator of San Marco in 1775. Andrea had been procurator in Padua, ambassador at Constantinople and Rome, and when Doge Renier died at the height of the Carnival, he was a candidate for the dogeship. He was well-known for his intellectual studies and meditations (he catalogued and published the letters of his tutor Carlo Lodoli), but he was equally well-known for his frivolous and libertine lifestyle, which was typical of the eighteenth century. As a young man he was a friend of Giacomo Casanova. With Casanova he indulged in every sort of merriment, including high society balls and intrigues, and the two also shared the favours of a damsel much-talked-about in the Venetian society of the day, Giustiniana Wynne, whom we have already encountered at the Palazzo Loredan dell'Ambasciatore. This young woman was madly in love with Andrea Memmo. While she experienced a soaring passion for him, he retained no more than a few pleasant memories of her. Giustiniana in fact never stopped thinking about her great love, even after many a gallant adventure and her marriage to Count Philip Orsini Rosenburg, the imperial ambassador. The subsequent friendship between Andrea and Giustiniana is recorded in voluminous sheafs of letters, which have not been published to this day.

Andrea Memmo passed away in his palace on the Grand Canal in 1793. The building remained in the hands of the Memmo family until the nineteenth century, when it was purchased by the Martinengos.

49 - Palazzo Michiel dalle Colonne

The name of this palace is derived from the columns which support the ground floor portico and which already existed when the Grimani family had the residence built in Venetian Byzantine style. The Zen family purchased the building towards the end of the seventeenth century, and hired the architect Antonio Gaspari to design a new Baroque façade.

Not long after this, the palace was acquired by Ferdinando Carlo Gonzaga, duke of Mantua. The duke was renowned for his passion for women, "especially if they were tall and fat." In Mantua he kept a seraglio, presided over by Countess Calori, and during the Carnival, he would take all his ladies to Venice. In 1706, when the Austrians conquered Mantua during the War of Spanish Succession, Ferdinando took refuge in his palace on the Grand Canal, and he took his collection of statues and paintings with him. He died in 1708 in Padua. His heirs sold the building to the counts Conigli of Verona who in turn sold it to Marcantonio Michiel, ancestor of the husband of Giustina Renier.

Giustina Renier, granddaughter of the second to last doge of Venice, was a brilliant and cultured woman. She even achieved a status as an author with her essay "Sull'origine delle feste veneziane," a valuable work that contains much information about religious and civil festivals in the age of the Serenissima. She also spoke French extremely well. Chateaubriand, an habitué at her salon, listened to his own declaration that Venice was "a city against nature" being argued against in perfect French.

In the nineteenth century, ownership of the palace passed to the Martinengos, who in turn bequeathed it to the Donà delle Rose. After having served as the offices of the Fascist Party and then as the premises of trade union organizations, the palace now houses the Registry Office.

From left to right: the palaces Michiel dalle Colonne, Michiel,
(end of the seventeenth century) and Michiel del Brusà
(rebuilt after a fire at the end of the eighteenth century).

50 - Palazzo Michiel del Brusà

In 1774 the negligence of a "serving-maid" started a fire which lasted for three whole days and destroyed almost the entire palace. From that day on, the old residence was called del Brusà, *brusà* meaning burnt. It was rebuilt with the help of the Republic in the original Gothic style. It remained in the hands of the Michiel family until the late nineteenth century.

51 - Palazzo Mocenigo, known as Il Nero

The Mocenigos, who originally came from Milan, provided the Republic of Venice with many generals, ambassadors, procurators of San Marco, and seven doges. Tommaso Mocenigo defeated the Turks in 1395, Pietro laid waste to the coastal regions of Asia and Greece in the latter half of the fifteenth century, and Lazzaro sank the Ottoman fleet in 1617 – the latter died while attempting to force a passage through the Dardanelles to attack Constantinople. It was under the dogeship of Alvise Mocenigo that the last Bucintoro, the Bucentaur, was built in 1727. This magnificent galley was used by the doge for official events, but most of all for wedding ceremonies at sea. It was Pope Alexander III who, in 1177, presented the doge with a gold ring with the auspicious remark that "the sea is your subject just as the bride is the bridegroom's." On Ascension Day, just outside the port of the Lido, a vase filled with holy water was thrown into the sea and after it the doge dropped the ring and pronounced the solemn words: "We marry you, O sea, as a sign of true and everlasting dominion."

This palace, attributed to Alessandro Vittoria, was erected in the sixteenth century on a previous Gothic construction. It remained the property of the Mocenigos until the extinction of the family at the end on the nineteenth century.

Following page : detail of the facade.

52 - Palazzo Mocenigo Casa Nuova

Built at the end of the sixteenth century and composed of two adjacent palaces, the Casa Nuova housed the great English Romantic poet, Lord George Byron, between 1818 and 1819. Shortly after Byron arrived in Venice on 10 November 1816, he found accommodation with a fabric merchant in Frezzeria and the first woman in Venice to enjoy his attentions was none other than the merchant's wife, Marianna Segati. Before very long, however, Byron decided to move to the Grand Canal. He took out a three-year lease on one of the most luxurious apartments on the canal, an entire floor in the Mocenigo palace.

This palace belonged to the branch nicknamed Casa Nuova, the part of the family that descended from Doge Giovanni and which included Alvise I, who was doge in 1571, the year of the victory at Lepanto. The master of the house was Alvise Francesco Mocenigo, grandson of Andrea Memmo (see Palazzo Memmo Martinengo). Alvise's mother was Lucietta Memmo, who apparently inherited from her father a certain appetite for licentious living. In speaking about Lucietta's clothing and attire, Effie Ruskin commented that there was good cause to thank the heavens that English ladies were not given to similarly spoiling their looks. It was Lucietta herself, who leased the palace to Byron. The rent, which included furnishings and linen, amounted to two hundred pounds a year. Thus Lord Byron moved into the Grand Canal in September 1818 with a domestic staff of fourteen, a butler, and a gondolier. His retinue also included two monkeys, a bear, two parrots, and a fox, and as Percy Bysshe Shelley noted during his visit to Venice, "the whole menagerie wandered around the apartments as if they all owned them." It was here that Byron wrote the first two cantos of *Don Juan*.

The English poet's amorous adventures in Venice were legion. He himself drew up a list for his friends Hobhouse and Kinnaird

Opposite: the inscription commemorating Byron's stay
in the Palazzo Mocenigo Casa Nuova, from 1818 to 1819.
Following double page: the main salon of the palace, furnished
with eighteenth-century pieces.

QVI
ABITÒ

LORD BYRON

DAL 1818
AL 1819

A CVRA DEL COMVNE DI VENEZIA
DEL BRITISH COVNCIL
E DELLA BYRON SOCIETY DI LONDRA

but without giving away any details. There was the singer Arpalice Tarruscelli, "the loveliest bacchante in the world," and a prostitute by the name of Da Mosti, who had given herself a patrician surname. Also, there were "Eleonora, Carlotta, Giulietta, the *Bolognese figurante* (an actress from Bologna), and la Santa, *cum multis aliis*." Nonetheless the woman who managed to keep a certain hold on him for a good two years was the famous Margherita Cogni, who was known as La Fornarina, because she was the wife of a baker. Byron and the twenty-two-year-old Venetian beauty had met one day while the poet was out riding with his friend Hobhouse, along the river Brenta. Her reputation was that of a somewhat vulgar woman, who was given to screaming and shouting and forever switching from furious fits of sobbing to bouts of wild laughter. She sincerely loved Byron, however, and showed him as much. One night the poet had been caught in a sudden storm while on a gondola. Upon returning home after struggling against the cloud burst, he found Margherita huddled on the stairs of the Palazzo Mocenigo Casa Nuova, waiting for him.

In this palace, Byron also got to know his last great love, the eighteen-year-old countess of Ravenna, Teresa Guiccioli. Lastly, Anne of Shaftesbury, wife of the Earl Marshal of England Thomas of Arundel, – the lady whose friendship had cost the life of Antonio Foscarini (see Palazzo Coccina Giunti Foscarini Giovannelli) – had also lived here.

The Casa Nuova branch of the Mocenigo family died out in 1877 and after changing hands several times, the building was divided up into apartments.

53 - Palazzo Mocenigo Casa Vecchia

This palace, which was built in the fifteenth century in the Gothic style of the day for the oldest branch of the house of Mocenigo, was completely renovated between 1623 and 1625 by Francesco Contin. The Mocenigos hailed from Milan and were in all probability descendants of the ancient Roman clan of the Cornelis. In 1574 the Palazzo Mocenigo was host to Emanuel Philibert of Savoy, victor at the battle of Mühlberg, and San Quintino who, upon leaving, presented the mistress of the house with a belt made of thirty golden rosettes, each with four pearls and a large jewel in the middle.

In 1591 and 1592 Giovanni Mocenigo opened the doors of his residence on the Grand Canal to the philosopher Giordano Bruno, who took refuge in Venice to escape persecution from the Church of Rome.

Disappointed that the philosopher did not reveal to him the secrets of alchemy and magic, Giovanni Mocenigo denounced him to the Venetian Inquisition and levelled a weighty charge of heresy against him. The philosopher had in fact made the mistake of remarking to Mocenigo that he was an enemy of the Mass and he had no time for any religion. He also said that Christ was a bleak figure whose "evil deeds" were aimed at stirring up the populace, and thus his condemnation probably did not come as a surprise. The senate decided to send him to Rome where he was tried over a period of seven years. Giordano Bruno refused to forsake his principles. He was tortured, found guilty of heretical teachings, and burnt at the stake on Campo dei Fiori in February 1600. Legend has it that his spirit still lives on in the Palazzo Mocenigo. It is said, even today, that the philosopher's ghost appears in the palace gardens every year on the anniversary of his death.

When the family died out in 1824, the palace changed hands several times and was divided up into apartments.

From left to right : the palaces Mocenigo Casa Nuova, Mocenigo Casa Vecchia,
and Contarini delle Figure.

54 - Palazzo Moro Lin

The "twelve-windowed palace" was built by the Tuscan painter Sebastiano Mazzoni, by linking together several already existing Gothic buildings via one central window. The first owner was Pietro Liberi, a painter who lived an adventurous life. He was born in Padua and after several years of apprenticeship in the studio of Padovanino, he set off for Constantinople. At Mitilini however the Turks took him prisoner and enslaved him. After eight months of imprisonment he managed to escape and flee to Malta, and then to Sicily. He then travelled round Europe, visiting Lisbon, Spain, and France, before spending three years in Rome, where he enthusiastically studied the work of Michelangelo and Raphael. Back in Venice, he became highly successful and founded the Collegio dei Pittori, an organization that eventually became part of the Accademia.

After the death of Pietro Liberi, the palace was acquired by the Lin family, grocers from Bergamo, who were admitted to the Venetian patriarchate in 1686. The Lins added a third floor and they also had the main salon painted with frescos. In 1748 as a result of the marriage between Gaspare Moro and Isabella Lin, the property passed to the Moro family.

In the early years of the nineteenth century, as the result of a strange request, the Palazzo Moro Lin was home to the Venetian painter Francesco Hayez, who set up his studio in the building. Later on, the building also accommodated another painter, Lodovico Lipparini, who is renowned for his refined portraits and his paintings inspired by the epic exploits of the Hellenes. He gave classes in the palace which were attended by artists and men of letters from Italy and abroad. Today the palace is divided up into various apartments.

55 - Palazzo Morosini Sagredo

On the façade of the palace, architectural features from the four-teenth-century Gothic period combine with features derived from the Oriental style that was fashionable in the following century. The windows on the mezzanine floor date back to the fourteenth century, while the three-lobe windows of the main floor are typical of the fifteenth century.

The building originally belonged to the Morosini family and was not acquired by the Sagredo family until the early eighteenth century. Eager to modernize the interior of his new abode on the Grand Canal, Gherardo Sagredo added a splendid main stairway at the far end of the atrium and covered the ceiling of the mezzanine with refined stuccowork. He also commissioned Pietro Longhi to make his one and only frescoed decoration, depicting the *Caduta dei giganti* (Fall of the Giants), inspired from the fantasies of Giulio Romano in the Palazzo Te in Mantua.

Like many Venetian families, the Sagredos were descendants of an ancient Roman clan from the imperial period, and their name, Sagredo, is explained by the fact that their forbears were often entrusted with special state secrets. As a result of services rendered, they became governors of Dalmatia and arrived in Venice in the ninth century. One of the most illustrious members of the family was Giovanni Sagredo, who was appointed state treasurer at the tender age of twenty-seven and who became ambassador to the court of Louis XIV of France and Charles II of England. He was eventually appointed procurator of San Marco.

The last descendant of the family, Agostino Sagredo, died in London in 1871. The old patrician residence is currently used as an office building.

56 - Ca' Pesaro

This palace, a masterpiece of Venetian Baroque, now houses the Museum of Modern Art and the Museum of Oriental Art – the initial inventories of the latter were formed by the collection that Enrico of Bourbon, count of Bardi, had amassed during his travels in Asia.

The building is the outcome of the mergence of three adjoining medieval palaces that were acquired by the Pesaros between 1558 and 1628, which is the year when work on the new palace got under way. The project was entrusted by Giovanni and Francesco Pesaro to Baldassare Longhena. However, construction of the palace actually continued until 1710, several years after the deaths of both Longhena and the Pesaros who had originally commissioned the work.

The Pesaro family had come to Venice in the mid-thirteenth century from the city in the Marches of the same name, where they were known by the surname of Palmieri. In Venice they were known as the Pesaro del Carro family, named after a wagon that they owned, which carried boats from the river Brenta to the lagoon close to Fusina.

One of the most illustrious members of the family was Jacopo Pesaro who, in 1519, charged Titian with the task of painting the family's famous altarpiece in the church of the Frari. Jacopo had been bishop of Paffo in Cyprus, and he was subsequently appointed papal envoy and general of the papal and Venetian troops involved in the war against the Turks.

Giovanni Pesaro, who commissioned the palace on the Grand Canal, had also been a general in the Venetian army in 1643 – this time, however, engaged against the papal army – and the story goes that he encouraged the sacking of private houses and the plunder of paintings and other works of art. Such rumours eventually had him hauled up before the courts.

In 1658 he was elected doge. During the conclave at which his election was decided upon, a little song did the rounds of Venice: "Viva el Pesaro dal caro che xe sta in preson per laro E per utima pazzia G'ha sposà dona Maria." (Long live Pesaro of the Wagon who was imprisoned for theft and to crown it all, went and married dona Maria.)

It was whispered abroad that, as the widower of Lucia Barbarigo, he had remarried the family governess, one Maria Santasofia.

Nonetheless the ups and downs of Giovanni's were nothing as tumultuous as those that beset his brother Leonardo. On 28 February 1601, during a wedding banquet at the Palazzo Minotto which degenerated into a free-for-all, Leonardo mortally wounded Sire Polo Lion, the official lover of the courtesan Lucrezia Baglioni. The Council of Ten stripped Leonardo of his noble title and property, and sent him into lifelong exile. He remained in exile for fifteen long years, but was allowed to return to Venice in 1616, on condition that he recruit, arm, and maintain at his own expense and for six months, one hundred soldiers.

One of his descendants, Francesco Pesaro, has gone down in history as the man who refused Napoleon's offer of an alliance with France. This duly triggered the declaration of war against Venice by the French and the subsequent fall of the Republic.

Pietro, the last member of the Pesaro family from the San Stae branch, emigrated to London and sold more than two hundred paintings from the family collection. After his death in 1830, Ca' Pesaro passed first to the Gradenigos, then to the duke of Bevilacqua of Verona, and lastly to the duke of la Masa, who was a general to boot. His wife left the property to the city of Venice, with the stipulation that it be used to organize exhibitions of young Venetian artists.

57 - Palazzo Pisani Gritti

Today in the Palazzo Pisani Gritti, the world-famous Gritti Palace Hotel, there is still a suite named after Ernest Hemingway, who was a devoted guest at the luxurious hotel during his many extended stays in Venice.

In addition to the American writer, the rooms of the Palazzo Pisani Gritti played host to another important man of letters; but this was when the building still belonged to Baroness Susanna Wetzlar. In May 1851 the baroness received John Ruskin and his young spouse Effie Gray. This was the second visit made by the Ruskins to the city, and John was in the thick of writing his book *The Stones of Venice*. His wife Effie had been greatly impressed and entertained by Baroness Wetzlar and by this "very curious old lady's" room, scented with essences. At the Palazzo Pisani Gritti, the baroness gave parties and balls, attended by the Venetian nobility, and the famous residence thus had a chance to recapture some of its former glory.

At the outset, this was the property of one of the wealthiest branches of the Pisani family, the Pisani dal Banco branch. The Gothic façade of the building, which dates back to the fourteenth century, was decorated with frescos painted by Giorgione, depicting various caprices of small *putti*, and four half-figures in the middle: Bacchus, Venus, Mars, and Mercury. Sadly, these outdoor frescos have completely vanished.

The palace passed to the Gritti family in 1814, when it was purchased by Camillo Gritti. Camillo's grandmother, Cornelia Barbaro Gritti, had been a poetess in Arcadia, by the name of Aurisbe Tarsense. By all accounts, she was a most beautiful woman, endowed with a sparkling sense of humour. She was also rumoured to have led a very busy love life. Sister of the poet Angelo Maria Barbaro and a great friend of Carlo Goldoni (who dedicated his play *Il Cavalier Giocondo* to her), she held a salon that was frequented by the most important men of letters of the day. Camillo Bernardino Gritti, Cornelia's son and father of the purchaser of the Palazzo Pisani, was also a poetry-lover and friend of writers such as Giuseppe Parini, who composed an ode in his honour.

The Gritti family went back a very long way indeed. In 1104 a certain Giovanni Gritti had been among the leading captains at the battle of Acri. Another Giovanni was elected archbishop of Corfu in 1360.

However Andrea Gritti, whose portrait now hangs in the Metropolitan Museum of Art in New York, was possibly the most famous member of this family and perhaps the greatest of the sixteenth-century doges. In his youth, he had been a merchant in Constantinople, then, a condottiere in the war against the League of Cambrai, and after that, a shrewd ambassador of the Republic.

In the nineteenth century, the Grittis sold their residence on the Grand Canal to Baroness Wetzlar. It was later transformed into a hotel.

58 - Palazzo Pisani

The Pisanis, noble bankers and businessmen, were the first people to set up a trading bank at Rialto in the fifteenth century. Between 1614 and 1615, Alvise Pisani had his new residence built in Campo Santo Stefano at a cost of two hundred thousand ducats. The work was entrusted to the architect Bartolomeo Manopola. The addition of the third floor and the construction of the library and the ballroom, were carried out in the first half of the eighteenth century by Girolamo Frigimelica and Bernardino Maccaruzzi. The ceiling of the salon was filled with Antonio Pellegrini's *Aurora e le ninfe dell'aria* (Dawn and the Nymphs of the Air) It is now housed at Biltmore in North Carolina, USA, while the Paolo Veronese ceiling with Jupiter, Juno, Cybele, and Neptune had been moved to Berlin and was later destroyed in the 1945 bombing of the city.

The Palazzo Pisani was famous for its grandiose receptions and parties, wherein guests would dance until daybreak. To mark the election of Almorò IV Zan Francesco as procurator of San Marco, the palace was decked out and illuminated and "the quality of the players in several different orchestras" dumbfounded the Venetians. Further, "for three days and the best part of three nights the streets leading to Campo di Santo Stefano were filled with crowds of people" receiving an "endless handout of wine" and bread.

Just as memorable were the festivities organized in honour of Gustavus III of Sweden, who travelled to Venice in 1784. Almorò I Alvise had the palace opulently decorated and he increased the lighting with lovely Murano lamps and purchased expressly for the sovereign, a solid gold table service. At the supper (which was served up by 160 waiters) and the ball given in honour of the king, there were more than eight hundred guests. When the time came for Gustavus III to leave, he admitted to Almorò that

he would never have been able to receive him with such pomp and circumstance in Stockholm. And the merrymaking continued. It is hardly surprising to learn, therefore, that the Pisanis' were in a state of financial crisis. After the fall of the Republic, all the family goods were put up for sale for their creditors.

The last descendant of the Pisani family, Almorò II, husband of Evelina van Millingen, whose father had tended to Lord Byron as he lay dying at Missolonghi, managed to buy back an apartment in the palace, which was now divided up among a handful of proprietors.

It was not until 1940 that the city of Venice was able to embark on a radical restoration of the palace, having at last come into full possession of the building. At the present time the palace houses the Benedetto Marcello Music Conservatory.

59 - Palazzo Pisani Moretta

The Gothic façade of the Palazzo Pisani Moretta, which is reminiscent of that of the Doge's Palace, includes one of the most beautiful mullioned windows with four lights on the Grand Canal. The two doorways point clearly to the fact that the building was inhabited by two different families belonging to the same line of the Pisani family. The house of Pisani descended from Nicolò Pisani, a member of the Higher Council from 1307 to 1328. The Pisani dal Banco branch of the family descended from his son Bertucci, the name dal Banco referring to the family's banking and trading activities, while the Santo Stefano branches descended from the other son Almorò (see Palazzo Pisani), as did the Santa Maria Zobenigo and Moretta branches.

The Pisanis, whose origins can be traced back to the counts Bassi of Pisa, were one of the wealthiest families in Venice. In addition to their palaces in the city, they owned two villas built by Andrea Palladio, one at Bagnolo, the other at Montagnana, plus a third villa built by Vincenzo Scamozzi at Lonigo.

After the death of Francesco, the last descendant of the Pisani Moretta line, the entire inheritance went to his daughter Chiara, who had married a Pisani dal Banco. She embarked upon a thorough overhaul of her residence at San Polo with the addition of a main staircase and decorations by two much sought-after artists of the day, Giovan Battista Piazzetta and Giambattista Tiepolo. Piazzetta painted the *Death of Darius*, now hanging in Ca' Rezzonico, while Tiepolo painted *Venus and Mars*.

One of Chiara's sons, Vettor, was a much talked-about character in the latter half of the eighteenth century. In 1753 Vettor had struck up a relationship with a young woman belonging to the Venetian petty bourgeoisie. She was called Teresa Vedova or Dalla Vedova, and was the daughter of a well-known engraver of mirrors. But the affair was discovered and Teresa was committed by

Following page: frescos by Giambattista Tiepolo painted in 1742 in the small salon.

her father to the boarding school of the convent of San Giacomo di Murano. The two lovers still managed to see one another however, thanks to the kindheartedness of the mother superior of the convent, and in 1758 they were secretly married. When this clandestine marriage was discovered, Teresa was sent by the state inquisitors to a convent where, not long after, she gave birth to a child. The young Pisani was reluctant to recognize this child and attempted to procure for Teresa a husband of convenience, but this was something she refused to contemplate. After obtaining the religious annulment of the marriage, Vettor remarried, this time with a Grimani. Teresa also remarried. In 1775 Vettor Pisani died, and the son born to him and Teresa came out of hiding and put forward his claims to the inheritance. All of Venice eagerly followed the court case of the century, and it was the boy who attracted the sympathies of patricians and the populace alike. When the court decided in favour of Pietro, he was escorted home by a triumphal procession of boats bedecked with laurel. He duly became the count of Bagnolo and was admitted to the Venetian patriciate.

Today the palace still belongs to the heirs of Pietro Pisani.

The *portego* of the main floor.

60 - Palazzo Priuli

A strange tale links Prince Eugene of Savoy with this palace in Campo Santa Maria Formosa.

In the early years of the eighteenth century, in the pandemonium of a "bull-hunt," Almorò Morosini was attacked in Campo Santa Maria Formosa by four masked men. He held off his assailants until help arrived, and in the meantime he even managed to slay a dog that was set upon him. Prince Eugene of Savoy watched the whole episode from a window in the Palazzo Priuli, and impressed by such bravado, he was keen to get to know Almorò Morosini. As a gift, he gave him a valuable painting by Correggio.

The building is attributed to the architect Bartolomeo Manopola, who built it for the Ruzzini family towards the end of the sixteenth century. The Ruzzinis had moved from Constantinople in the tenth century, and were one of Venice's oldest families. The most illustrious member of the house was Carlo. Ambassador in Spain, Vienna, and Constantinople, he was eventually elected doge in 1732, at the age of almost eighty. He had a particular passion for classical antiquities, books, codices, and paintings. His picture gallery at San Giobbe contained more than 160 works of art. However, this did not mean that he ever actually lived in the palace planned by Manopola, though it was he who made provision for his heirs to reside in the building at Campo Santa Maria Formosa, along with their relatives, the Loredans. When the Loredans died out, the property reverted in its entirety to the Ruzzinis.

In 1801 after the fall of the Republic, the patrician residence passed to Pietro Priuli. Today, sad to say, it is uninhabited and in a state of neglect.

61 - Palazzo Priuli all'Osmarin

This venerable fourteenth-century palace situated on the Rio
all'Osmarin – whose façade was once decorated with frescos by
Palma the Elder – was extended towards the Rio di San Severo
in the fifteenth century, a period when the famous mullioned
windows with two lights were built.

The Priuli family, Hungarian aristocrats who came to Venice as
diplomats were admitted to the patriciate in about 1100. They
provided Venice with three doges and a clutch of cardinals,
prelates, procurators, and generals.

After the fall of the Serenissima, the Palazzo Priuli all'Osmarin
became the property of two quite separate families, the Farsettis
and the Mocenigo Alvisopolis. Today it is divided up into several apartments.

62 - Palazzo Querini Benzon

The famous popular song "La Biondina in gondoleta" (The Fair-haired Lass in the Gondola), set to music by Simone Mayr, was originally written by the Venetian poet Antonio Lamberti in honour of Marina Querini Benzon, who held one of the most celebrated of eighteenth century literary salons here in her residence on the Grand Canal. The most dazzling Parisian salons were "stupid and dull in comparison with Signora Benzon's salon," wrote Stendhal. In addition to Stendhal, the palace, which was built in the first half of the eighteenth century, was frequented by Lord Byron, who also made very favorable mention of her salon, Thomas Moore, Chateaubriand, and Ugo Foscolo, with whom, in 1797, Marina had danced half-naked. Chateaubriand, however, was too shy to take part in the soirées hosted by the exuberant mistress of the house. He remained glued to a seat away in a corner, and despite the efforts of Countess Marina, never managed to find a lady who would entertain him. At midnight, the poet would leave in his "silent, solitary gondola" and return to the Hôtel de l'Europe.

It was said that Marina Querini Benzon was not ashamed of sending out invitations to handsome young men whom she had glimpsed in the city. She was even accused of having an incestuous relationship with her son Vittore, who died of consumption at a tender age. Moreover it was whispered that the noblewoman had not even closed her salon on the day of her son's death.

In her old age she grew huge, so huge in fact that she earned the nickname Stramozzo Despontà (Unstitched Mattress).

The palace of the Querini Benzons, which had known so many men of letters and other illustrious figures, passed into other hands when the family died out.

63 - Ca' Rezzonico

In his disdain for Baroque architecture, John Ruskin regarded Ca'
Rezzonico as the most stupid of palaces, with no variety of mea-
surement and no harmoniously placed stones. For him, it was
the only building he knew in Venice that was as ugly as those
being newly built at that time. But it had a quite different effect
on Henry James who remained fascinated by this majestic temple of the baroque, admirable in its order, and he likened it to a
mythological sea horse with its wide chest and its rampant knees
represented by the water stairs.

The construction of Ca' Rezzonico was embarked upon in the
latter half of the seventeenth century by Baldassare Longhena
for Filippo Bon; but it was interrupted for more than fifty years,
and was not completed until the eighteenth century by Giorgio
Massari for Giambattista Rezzonico, the new owner. The architect took up Longhena's plan, but nevertheless made slight
adaptations in order to meet the taste of the eighteenth century; thus *putti* embellish the façade, plumed warrior heads and
women with knotted braids were placed at the top of the arches,
and supple reeds and ears of corn decorated the oval windows
and walls. The interior decoration was entrusted to the most famous artists and decorators of the century, such as Giambattista
Tiepolo, Jacopo Guarana, and Gaspare Diziani. Not surprisingly,
Ca' Rezzonico became one of the most luxurious of all the patrician houses.

The feast given for the marriage of Lodovico Rezzonico and
Faustina Savorgnan in 1758 is evoked in the nuptial allegory
painted by Tiepolo on the ceiling of one of the rooms. Feasts
and parties were held so regularly (receptions were given to mark
the election of Pope Clement XIII in 1758, and in honour of the
duke of York, brother of King George III of England in 1764)
that even the colossal fortune of the Rezzonicos could not cope

The ballroom with frescos by Giambattista Crosato.

with the expenditure. The heirs of the last Rezzonico, who died in 1810, had to sell the residence.

After being bought by a succession of new owners, Ca' Rezzonico was finally purchased in 1888 by the English poet Robert Browning, who died shortly after his acquisition while he was out walking at the Lido. Attesting to the poet's sojourn, the words, "Open my heart and you will see graven inside of it Italy," are still visible on the façade. The palace has been in the hands of the city of Venice since 1930, and today it houses the Museum of Eighteenth-Century Venetian Art.

64 - Palazzo Soranzo

Originally decorated with frescos painted by Giorgione, the façade of the Palazzo Soranzo in Campo San Polo appears to represent an exception to the Venetian rule whereby the main façade of a building must give on to water. In reality, old prints and maps show that a *rio* did exist here. Even today it is still possible to discern the outlines of the channel, which was buried in 1761, in the stone paving in front of the palace.

One of the most illustrious guests to stay at the Palazzo Soranzo was Dante Alighieri who, in his capacity as ambassador of the Polentaris, lords of Ravenna, was received by Doge Giovanni Soranzo in his private residence.

In 1548 Campo San Polo was the scene of a tragic event: the assassination of Lorenzino de'Medici, who had taken refuge in Venice, under the name of Messer Dario, after killing his cousin Alessandro, duke of Florence.

To this day, the palace is still owned by the Soranzo family.

65 - Palazzo Tron

The sixteenth-century Palazzo Tron is associated above all with
the memory of Andrea Tron and his wife Caterina Dolfin. Andrea
was an ambassador in Paris, Vienna, Madrid, and the Hague and
then, as procurator of San Marco, he had done his utmost to
pump new life back into the age-old seafaring Republic and to
champion the resumption of Venetian trade, which had been on
the decline. Already well on in years, he fell head over heels in
love with Caterina, an impoverished patrician lady who was married to an impoverished member of the Tiepolo family. Andrea
began as her devoted admirer, and later became her lover. After
the annulment of his first marriage, he married her in 1772.
Caterina was pretty, high-spirited, witty, and cultured. She had
close friendships with many intellectuals and men of letters, and
became a very influential patron of the Venetian literary world.
Her salon was attended by the most illustrious figures in Europe,
and her progressive ideas were well-known, so much so, in effect, that the Inquisitors ordered that her salon be closed down
for harbouring *strissimi studiosi, citavimo Russò* (most illustrious
scholars, such as Rousseau).

As generous as she could be with her favourite friends, she was
also capable of being just as unfriendly and perfidious towards
anyone not to her liking. For instance, she had the secretary of
the senate, Pierantonio Gratarol, her rebuffed admirer, poked
fun at by a company of comic actors, with a play titled *Le droghe
d'Amore* (The Drugs of Love). Everybody was able to recognize
the secretary in the character of Don Adone, a trifling fop and
ladies' man. The play was so successful that Gratarol, who was
mocked and even chased through the Piazza San Marco by hordes
of small boys, was actually forced to leave Venice.

Nonetheless Caterina was an excellent hostess and was able to
show off these talents when in 1775, she received a visit from

the Holy Roman Emperor, Joseph II, son of Maria Theresa of Habsburg. The palace was lit up by day with magnificent lamps and silver candelabra, and the ball lasted until dawn. In addition, it was probably in honour of the emperor that Andrea Tron commissioned Giacomo Guarana to paint the ballroom with the fresco known as *The Fall of the Giants*.

The palace had only just been enlarged – with the addition of two wings and the construction of the *casin* (a garden pavillion), in which a magnificent ballroom had been installed – when the *casin* was destroyed in 1828, after the death of the last family member, Cecilia Tron.

Cecilia, daughter of Renier Zen and wife of Francesco Tron, was an intelligent and lively woman, much admired by visitors to her salon, for her beauty. In addition to being well known as a supporter of the arts and sciences, she was also renowned for her amorous adventures. The most famous of these was her relationship with the notorious count Cagliostro, with whom she only broke off when the count was forced to flee the city. Apparently, promising to reveal the secret of transforming lead into gold, he had tricked a wealthy merchant out of one thousand gold coins. With the fall of the Republic, Cecilia became a francophile and Jacobin, and in September 1797 her palace was the setting for a huge "democratic" feast. She received Josephine Bonaparte in a gondola at Mestre and with the arrival of the Austrians, she was suspected of being revolutionary. But she refused to be intimidated, carried on with her life, continued to hold her salon, and took as her second husband her devoted admirer Count Giorgio Ricchi.

On her death, the immense wealth of the Trons, which also included a palace at Sant'Eustachio, passed on to her daughter, Chiara Maria. At the present time the famous residence houses the faculty of architecture of the University of Venice.

66 - Ca' Vendramin Calergi

It was in 1481 that Andrea Loredan purchased a modest building alongside the church of San Marcuola, where he began to
construct a palace whose magnificence would attract the admiration of everyone – "a house on the Grand Canal worthy of
being respected and honoured, with a façade that would be the
loveliest in all of Venice." The palace – work upon which spanned
the period from 1481 to 1509, with various interruptions – is attributed to the architect from Mauro Codussi of Bergamo. While
lavish buildings were still being constructed in the late Gothic
style, this architect stood apart from the rest by adopting a new
classical vocabulary.

This palace was known by the name of Non Nobis because of the
words *Non nobis Domine* and *Non nobis* inscribed on the façade;
this being the motto of the proudest of all religious orders, that
of the Knights Templar. Behind this façade covered with multi-
colored marble, the building contained an entrance hallway
painted with frescos by Giorgione, a painting by Raphael, and
from 1530 onwards, Giorgione's famous *Tempest* also hung in
the palace.

In 1614 the new proprietor, Vincenzo Grimani had a wing added
to the building. However, in 1658, the Grimani brothers were
accused of sundry conspiracies and crimes and duly executed.
Their property was threatened with destruction, but in the end
of the day, on account of the beauty of the building, only the
new wing was razed to the ground. By way of symbolic humil-
iation, a column was then built, but it was demolished two years
later, after which the wing was rebuilt.

The palace then passed by turns into the hands of the Vendramin
family and of Duchess Marie Caroline du Berry (who had a three
hundred seat theatre built into it, where Venetian high society
could give performances before a royal audience). In 1870 the

Opposite and page 195: gambling salons of the casino
in Palazzo Vendramin Calergi.

building became the property of the heirs of Marie Caroline's second husband, the Sicilian count Enrico Lucchesi-Palli.

A decade later, in 1882, after the triumph of *Parsifal* at Bayreuth, Richard Wagner rented twenty rooms in the palace. Franz Liszt, whose daughter Wagner had married, joined him in November of that same year and it was there that he composed his work *La lugubre gondola*. On Christmas eve 1882, the two great composers gave a private concert in the La Fenice theatre. However Wagner did not have a chance to live for very long in the Ca' Vendramin Calergi, for he died in 1883 in a bedroom on the mezzanine situated in the garden wing – this room, which today lies empty, still has the wallpaper chosen by Wagner.

According to legend, Giuseppi Verdi was in Venice at the same time and wanted to pay tribute to the maestro, whom he so admired, on the very afternoon of that tragic day.

In memory of Wagner, the dukes of Lucchesi-Palli organized concerts of Wagnerian music every year in the garden, and on the low wall right beside the immense palace, Gabriele d'Annunzio had a stone affixed, bearing the following words: "In this palace / the last breath of Richard Wagner / was heard by souls / forever / like the tide lapping against marble."

Ca' Vendramin Calergi, which has been the property of the city of Venice since 1956, currently houses the casino.

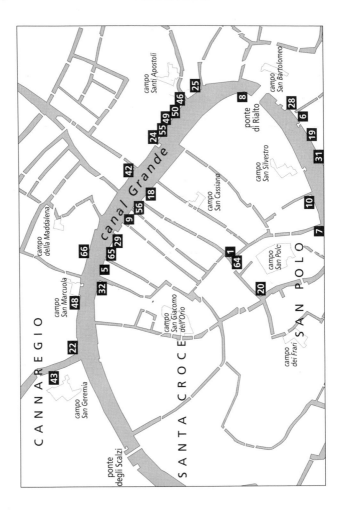

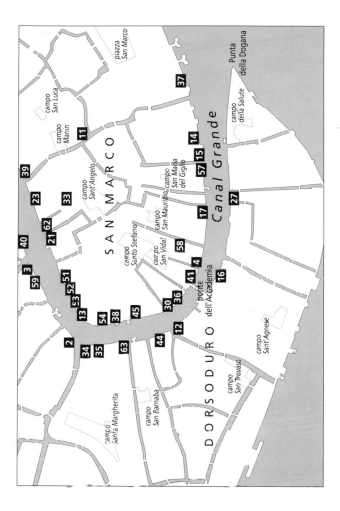

Bibliography

Aldegnani, Gianluca, *Le corti: spazi pubblici e privati nella città di Venezia*, Cittastudi, Milan, 1991.

Bassi, Elena, *Palazzi di Venezia; Admiranda Urbis Venetae*, la Stamperia di Venezia Editrice, Venice, 1976.

Chiappini, Ileana, *Palazzo Pisani Moretta. Economia, arte, vita sociale di una famiglia veneziana nel dociottesimo secolo*, Franco Maria Ricci, Milan, 1983.

Civiltà veneziana del Quattrocento, collective work, Sansoni, Florence, 1957.

Civiltà veneziana del Rinascimento, collective work, Sansoni, Florence, 1958.

Cunaccia, Cesare M., *Venice, hidden splendors*, Flammarion, Paris, 1994

Damerini, Gino, *Settecento veneziano. La vita, i tempi, gli amori, i nemici di Caterina Dolfin Tron*, Mondadori, Milan, 1939.

Fontana, Gianjacopo, *Venezia monumentale. I palazzi*. Filippi Editore, Venice, 1967.

Foscari, Lodovico, *Affreschi esterni a Venezia*, Hoepli, Milan, 1936.

Franzoi, Umberto, *The Grand Canal,* Vendome Press, New York, 1997.

Fremder, Laura, Guanti, Giovanni (under the direction of), *Venezia curiosa, esoterica, minimale*, Guanti, Milan, 1990.

Guida ai misteri e segreti di Venezia e del Veneto, collective work, Sugar, Milan, 1970.

Lauritzen, Peter, Zielcke, Alexander, *Palaces of Venice*, Lawrence King Publishing, London, 1979.

Mc Andrew, John, *L'Architettura veneziana del primo Rinascimento*, Marsilio, Venice, 1983-1995.

Molmenti, Pompeo, *Curiosità di storia veneziana*, Zanichelli, Bologna, 1918.

Romanelli, Giandomenico, Pedrocco, Filippo, *Ca' Rezzonico*, Guide Artistiche Electa, Electa, Milan, 1995.

Romanelli, Giandomenico, Pavanello, Giuseppe, *Palazzo Grassi*, Albrizzi, Venice, 1986.

Romanelli, Giandomenico, *Portrait of Venice*, Rizzoli, New York, 1997.

Ruskin, John, *The Stones of Venice*, Da Capo, New York, 1985.

Salvadori, Antonio, *Architect's guide to Venice*, Butterworths, London, 1990.

Tassini, Giuseppe, *Aneddoti storici veneziani*, Filippi, Venice, 1965.

Tassini, Giuseppe, *Curiosità veneziane*, Fuga Editore, Venice, 1915.

Valcanover, Francesco, *Ca' d'Oro. La Galleria Giorgio Franchetti*, Guide Artistiche Electa, Electa, Milan, 1994.

Venezia e dintorni, collective work, Touring Club Italiano, Milan, 1951.

Venezia e Parigi, collective work, Elacta, Milan, 1989.

Venezia e Veneto, collective work, Hoepli, Milan, s.d.

Viaggiatori stranieri a Vanezia, collective work, acts of the Congress of the Ateneo Veneto, October 13-15, 1979. Texts collcted by Emanuele Kanceff and Gaudenzio Boccazzi; University Center of Slatkine, Moncalieri, Geneva, 1981.

Zorzi, Alvise, *Canal Grande*, Rizzoli, Milan, 1994.

Zorzi, Alvise, *Venetian Palaces*, Rizzoli, New York, 1990.

POCKET ✒ ARCHIVES
HAZAN